NUFFIEL
NATIONAL CURRICULUM
MATHEMATIC

Shape, space and measures 2

NC LEVEL 5
GCSE FOUNDATION

Heinemann

Project director: Peter Reynolds
Assistant director: Mike Cornelius
Project manager: Jan Hoare

Author of this book
Geoff Fowler with additional material by Rosemary Flower and Alison Jefferson
Edited by Peter Reynolds

Heinemann Educational
a division of Heinemann Publishers (Oxford) Ltd,
Halley Court, Jordan Hill, Oxford, OX2 8EJ

OXFORD LONDON EDINBURGH
MADRID ATHENS BOLOGNA PARIS
MELBOURNE SYDNEY AUCKLAND SINGAPORE TOKYO
IBADAN NAIROBI HARARE GABORONE
PORTSMOUTH NH (USA)

First published 1995

95 96 97 98 10 9 8 7 6 5 4 3 2 1

ISBN 0 435 50546 7

Designed and typeset by Ken Vail Graphic Design
Illustrated by James Alexander, Rupert Besley, Paul Cookson, Nick Hawken, David Holmes, Hussein Hussein, Sue King, Mike Lacey, Nigel Paige, Graeme Morris (Ken Vail Graphic Design)
Printed in Spain by Mateu Cromo, S.A. Pinto (Madrid)

Acknowledgements
The project and publishers gratefully acknowledge the contribution made by the late Hilary Shuard.
The authors and publishers would like to thank for permission to reproduce the following photographs and copyright material :
p. 61 Robert Harding Picture Library, Science Photo Library/David Parker;
p. 62 House of Commons/Jarrold Publishing.
Cover image: Ace Photo Agency
London Regional Transport for the reproduction of London Underground tube map.
HMSO for permission to reproduce the National Curriculum level descriptions.

Every effort has been made to contact copyright holders of material published in this book. Any omissions will be rectified in subsequent printings if notice is given to the publisher.

Cover picture
The volume of air in this balloon is about 77 000 cubic metres. Units 1 and 6 look at the volumes of solids and liquids and the different units we use to measure them.

About this book

This book is part of the Nuffield National Curriculum Mathematics series. It will help you learn mathematics and we hope you will enjoy using it.

How this book is organized

There are nine units of work in this book. They are numbered Unit 1 to Unit 9. Each unit provides information for you to read and questions and activities for you to do.

The units are presented in short sections. Each section has a letter and a title. For example, Section B of Unit 2 has the title:

B A piece of cake

The questions and activities in Section B are numbered **B1**, **B2**, **B3** and so on to help you find them easily.

The contents list on the next page shows you where each unit and section starts and tells you what mathematics they cover.

Symbols used in the Nuffield books

These symbols are shown in the margin of your book whenever you need worksheets, equipment or access to a computer:

S2:4

this means you need worksheet S2:4 from the Assessment and Resource Pack.

protractor
compass

you need equipment listed between the lines

spreadsheet

you need access to a computer and the software shown.

Contents

UNIT 1 Area and volume

A How long is a piece of string?

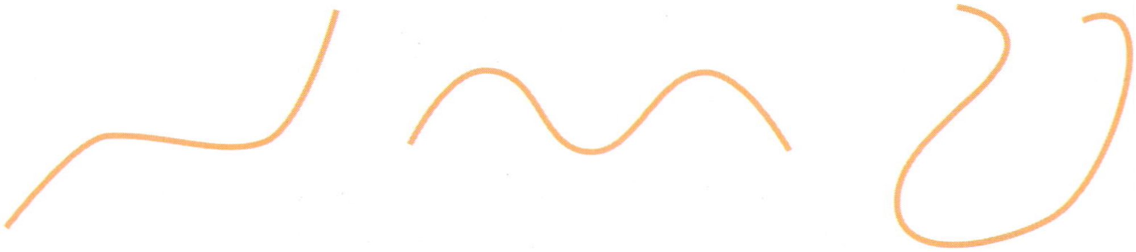

Which is the longest?

Guess which piece of string is the longest.

Then use a piece of string, or a strip of paper, to check if you are right.

A1 If the three pieces of string had been cut from one piece, how long would the original piece of string be?

A piece of string is made into a closed loop by taping the two ends together.

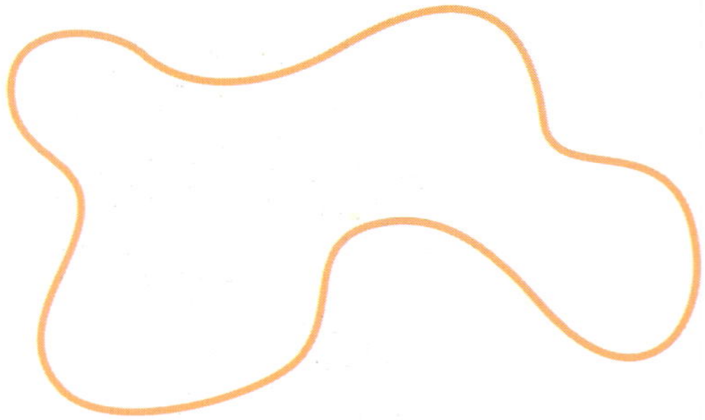

It is thrown three times in the air and each lands each time on centimetre squared paper as shown:

A2 **a** **b** **c**

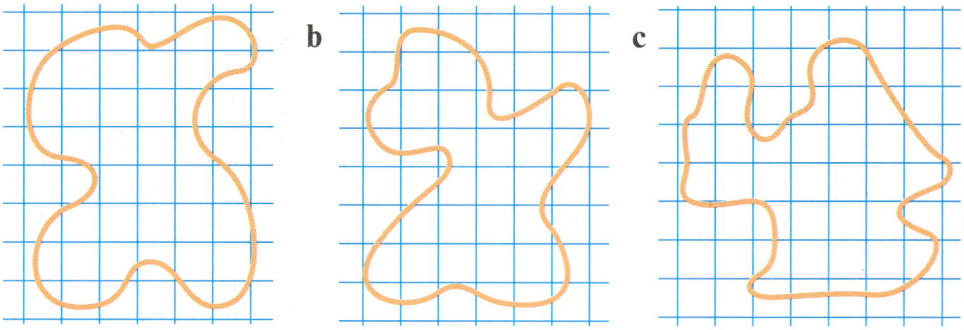

Count squares to work out the area enclosed each time.

A3 How did you count squares that were crossed by the string?

B Area by counting

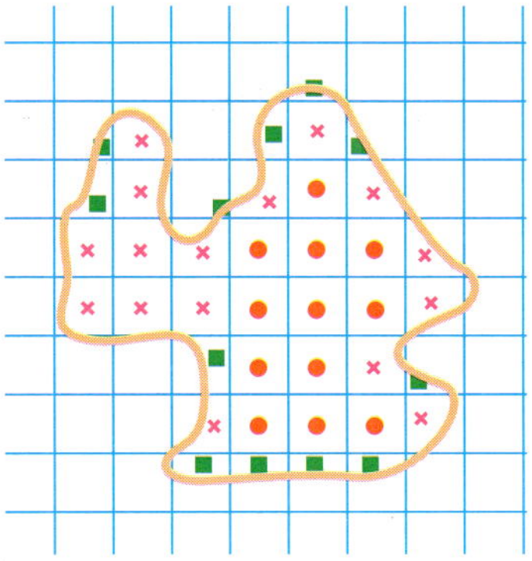

To find the approximate area of this shape: count the number of whole centimetre squares (marked with a dot).

Where the string cuts the square, count it as a whole square if more than half the square is inside the loop (marked with a cross).

Where less than half of the square is inside the loop (marked with a square) do *not* count it.

The area enclosed by the loop is about 12 + 16 = 28 square centimetres (cm^2).

B1 **a** Compare this answer with your answer to part **c** of question **A2**.

b Worksheet S2:1 has copies of parts **a** and **b** of question **A2**. With tracing paper make copies of parts **a** and **b** of question **A2** or use Worksheet S2:1. Use the method above to find the approximate areas of the two shapes and compare your answers with those you worked out before.

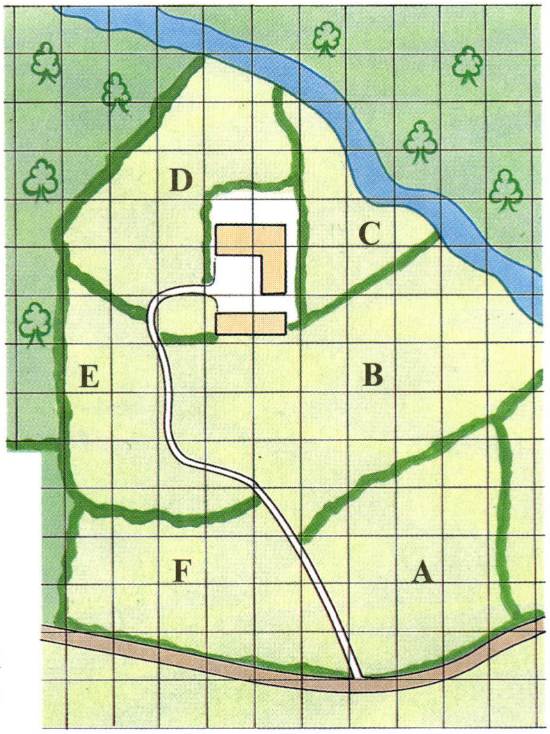

B2 Here is the plan of a farm drawn on squared paper. Each square is 10 m × 10 m.

a Using the plan of the farm on Worksheet S2:1, work out the area of each of the six fields.

b List the fields in order of size.

Counting squares can be used to find the **area of a rectangle**. If you have met this idea before the next question is a quick revision.

B3 Work out the area of these rectangles drawn on centimetre squared paper:

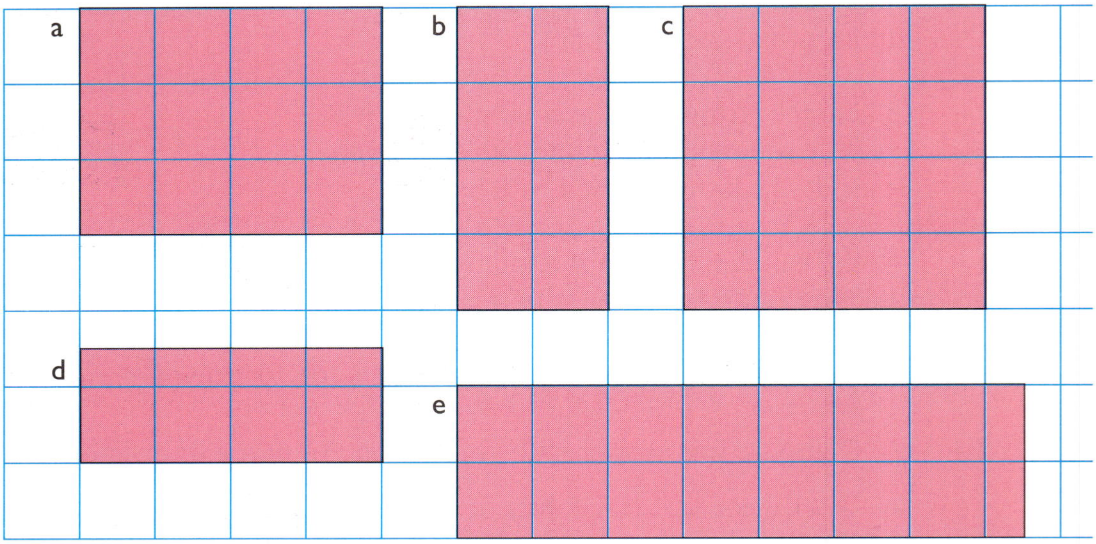

B4 Work out the area of this rectangle without drawing in the squares:

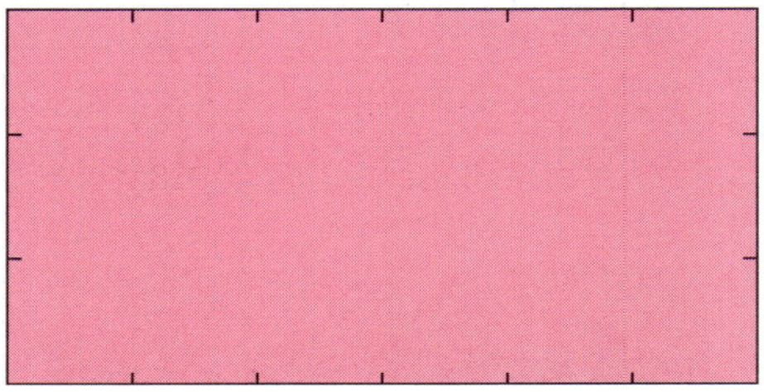

B5 Explain how you worked out the area in question **B4**.

You may have noticed that the rectangle in question **B4** can be split into 3 strips of 6 squares:

The area is $6 \times 3 = 18\,\text{cm}^2$.

This idea works for rectangles of any size.

The area is the number of squares in each row multiplied by the number of rows. So the area of a rectangle can be found using the rule:

Area of a rectangle = width × length

C Dicey rectangles

Dicey rectangles is a game for two or three players.

two dice
coloured pencils

You need two dice, an A5 (half A4) sheet of dotty square paper, a ruler and coloured pencils.

C1 Make a copy of the table:

Turn	Player A		Player B		Player C	
	Throw	Area	Throw	Area	Throw	Area
1						
2						
3						
10						

Draw a rectangular perimeter round your sheet of dotty paper. Each player chooses a different colour. Players take turns to throw the two dice which are recorded as width and length.

A rectangle is drawn with this width and length on the dotty paper and coloured with the player's colour. Each player has 10 turns.

If a rectangle will not fit on the dotty paper, then the player misses that turn. The winner is the player with the greatest total area covered.

Here is a game which has been started:

Turn	Player A		Player B		Player C	
	Throw	Area	Throw	Area	Throw	Area
1	6 × 4	24	2 × 1	2	3 × 5	15
2	4 × 3	12				
3						
10						

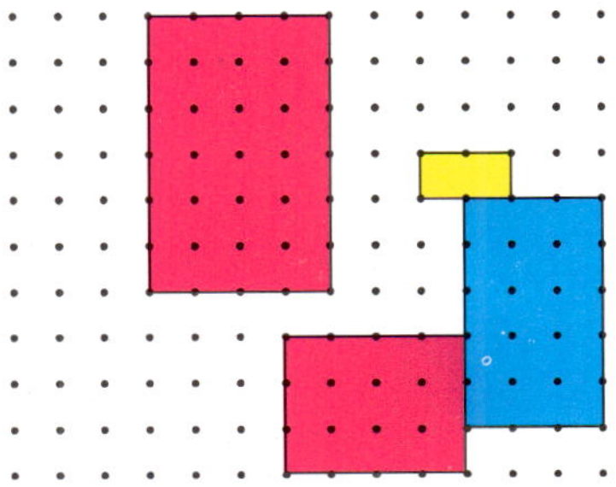

C2 Measure each rectangle below accurately in centimetres and work out its area. Repeat using millimetres.

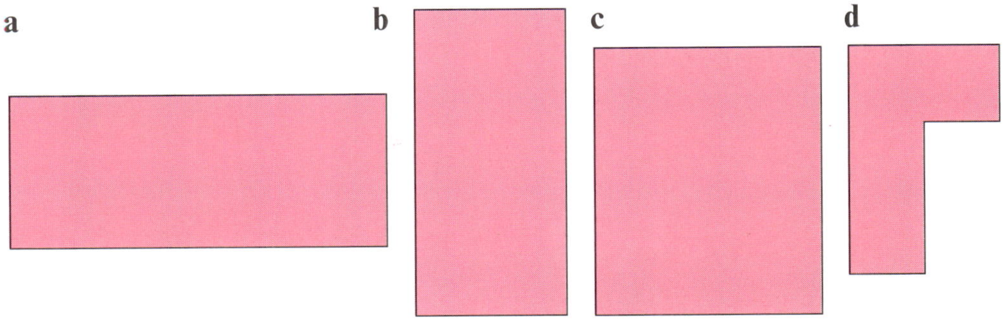

C3 Using your answers to question **C2**, how many $mm^2 = 1\ cm^2$?

D Areas and perimeters

square dotty paper

You need a sheet of square dotty paper, ruler and pencil.

On your sheet of dotty paper, draw five different rectangles, labelled A, B, C, D and E, that each have an area of $24\,cm^2$.

For each rectangle, work out the **perimeter** (the distance round the outside). Put all your results in a table like the one shown here.

	Rectangle	Perimeter
A	12 x 12	28cm
B		
C		
D		
E		

D1 What can you say about the rectangle with

a the longest perimeter

b the shortest perimeter?

D2 Using a perimeter of 24 cm, draw a rectangle of area $20\,cm^2$.

D3 **a** Using a perimeter of 24 cm, draw a rectangle of area $36\,cm^2$.

b What is the special name for this type of rectangle?

D4 Using a perimeter of 20 cm, draw a rectangle with area:

a $16\,cm^2$ **b** $24\,cm^2$ **c** $25\,cm^2$

D5 What is the largest possible area of a rectangle with a perimeter of 20 cm? What is this shape?

D6 A farmer is putting the sheep that he is taking to market in a special pen at the side of a field.

He is using the wall as one side of the pen and making the other three sides with 20 pieces of fencing, each one metre long.

a If he uses all 20 pieces of fencing how many different rectangular pens can he make? Make sketches of them.

b What is the largest area of field that he can enclose?

E Chocoblocks – a mathematician's delight

If you were a princess, which box would you choose?

Chocoblocks are little cubes of chocolate.

They come in lots of different sized boxes.

Three different sized boxes are shown here.

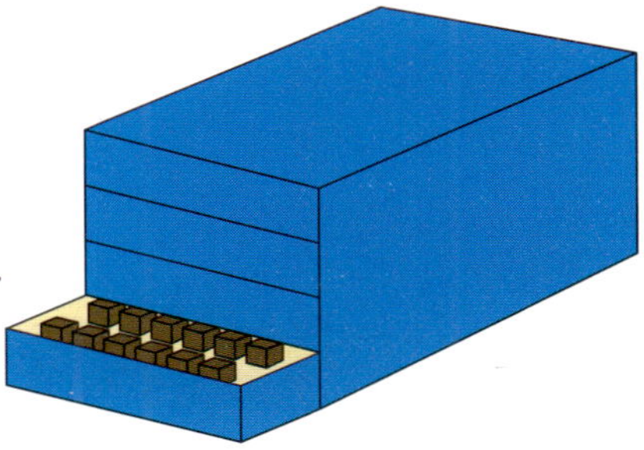

E1 Which box contains the most chocolate?
How many are there in each box?

This box has four drawers (or layers) in each drawer there are eight rows with six chocolates in each.

In the second box, there are only two layers, but in each layer there are ten rows with ten chocoblocks in each row.

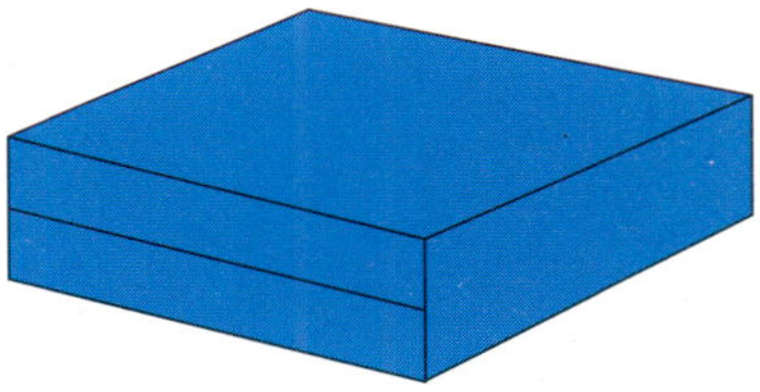

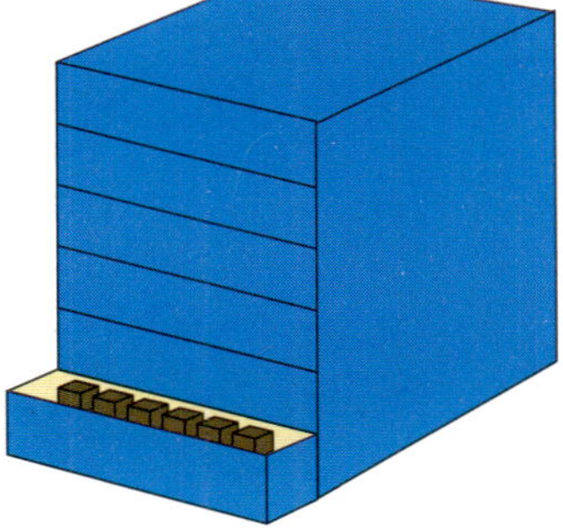

The third box is a cube box of chocoblocks. There are six drawers, each with six rows containing 6 chocoblocks.

To work out how many chocoblocks there were in each box (or **cuboid**), you need first to work out how many chocoblocks there are in each layer. Then you multiply this number by the number of layers.

For example, to find how many chocoblocks there are in this box:

In each layer, there are four rows of five chocoblocks.

That is, 4 × 5 = 20 chocoblocks.

There are two layers, each with 20 chocoblocks.

That is, 20 × 2 = 40 chocoblocks.

E2 Work out how many chocoblocks there are in each of these boxes:

a

b

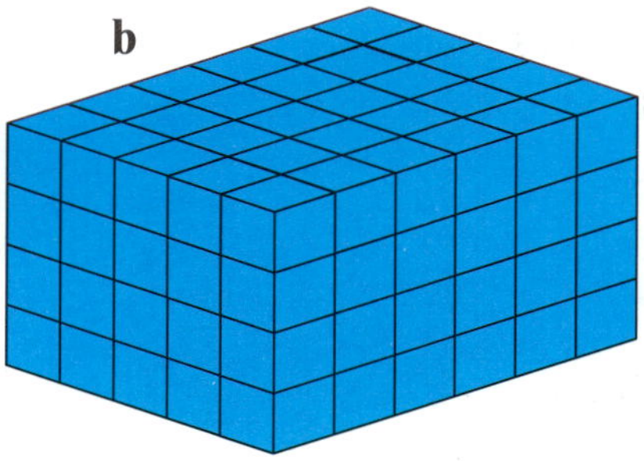

c

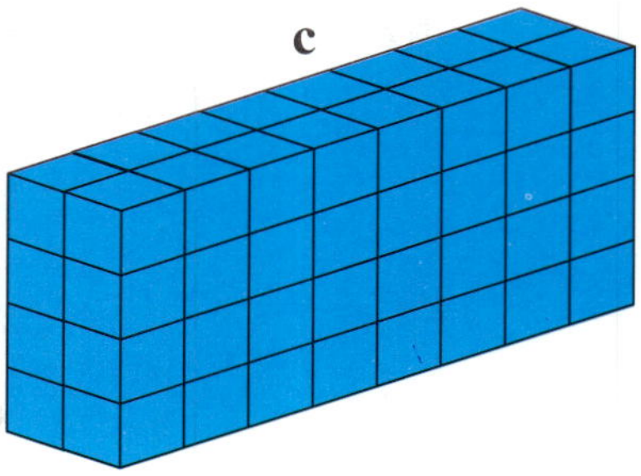

d

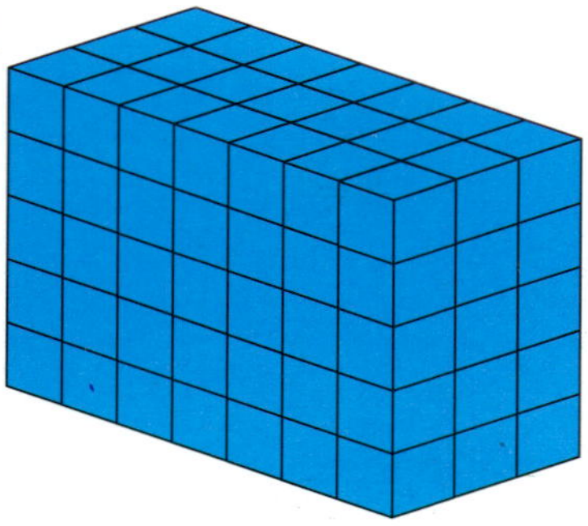

e

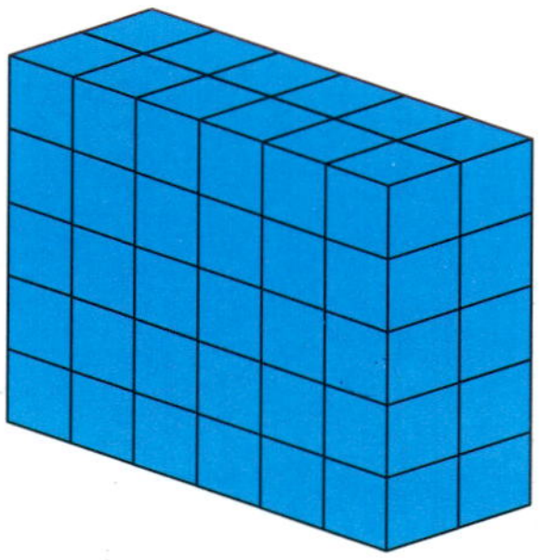

f

E3 Each layer of a mini-box of chocoblocks has four rows, with three chocoblocks in each row.
If there are 36 chocoblocks in a box, how many layers are there?

F Play bricks

24 small cubes
dotty triangle paper

You will need dotty triangle paper and 24 small cubes.

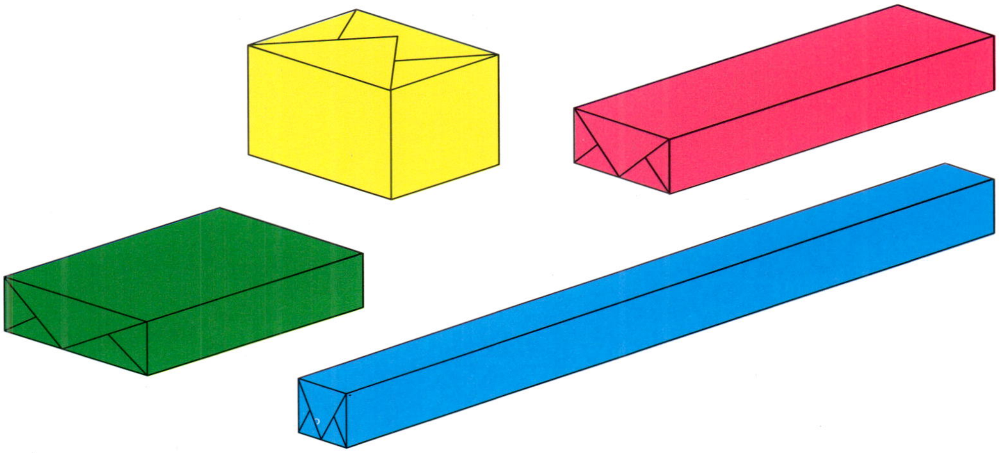

Each of the cuboids shown above contains 12 small cubes, but they have all been wrapped up.

F1 **a** Using twelve cubes, make each of the four packages.

b As you finish each of the packages draw it on dotty triangle paper.

F2 Now write the dimensions of each package under your drawings like this:

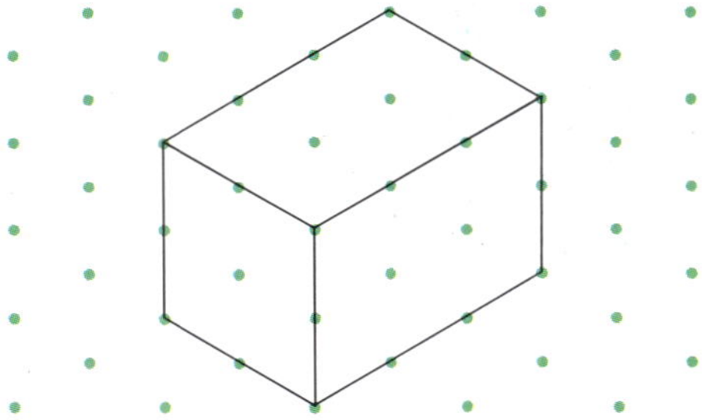

This is a 2 × 2 × 3 cuboid.

F3 Take 24 cubes and use all of them to make a cuboid.

a How many different cuboids can you make?

b Draw four of your cuboids on dotty triangle paper.

Write the dimensions underneath.

F4 Which of your cuboids do you think would make the best shape for a pack of 24 wooden bricks? Give your reasons.

G Volume

Too much volume!

In mathematics, we use the word volume for the bulk of material in a three-dimensional solid or for the amount of liquid.

We measure volume in cubes, for example, cubic centimetres (cm^3) or cubic metres (m^3).

For example, to find the volume of this cuboid:

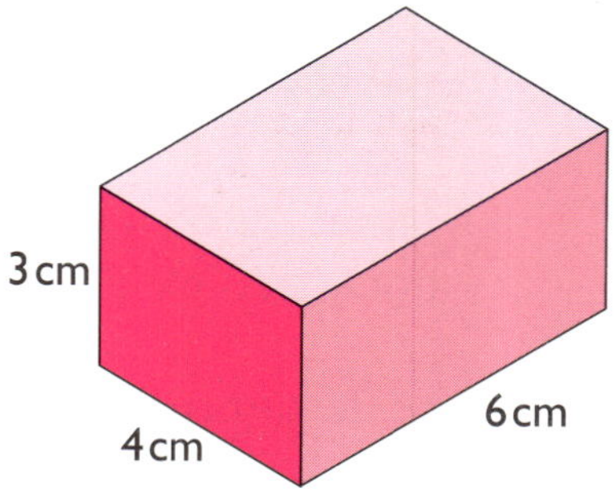

Volume = length × width × height

Volume = 6 cm × 4 cm × 3 cm
Volume = $72\,cm^3$

This means that to make this cuboid, you would need 72 of them.

G1 Use the rule, volume of cuboid = $l \times w \times h$, to calculate the volume of each of these cuboids where all measurements are in centimetres:

a $3 \times 5 \times 5$ **b** $2 \times 3 \times 6$ **c** $1\frac{1}{2} \times 2 \times 2$

d $3.5 \times 4 \times 5$ **e** $9 \times 1.4 \times 5$ **f** $7.2 \times 5 \times 2.5$

g $3.6 \times 3.6 \times 3.6$ **h** $5.2 \times 4.3 \times 7.9$

G2 The back of a lorry is full of sand which is level with the top of the sides.

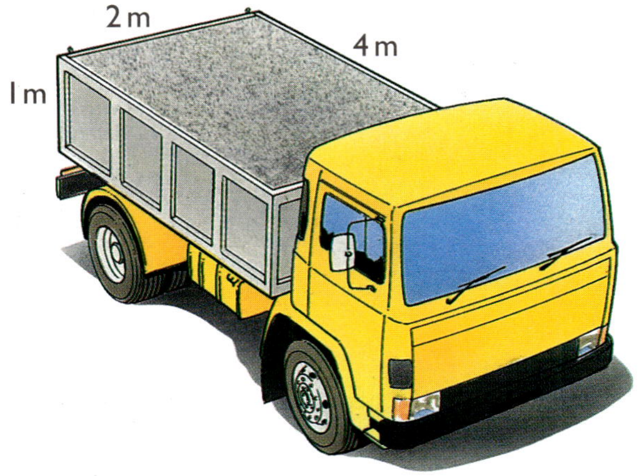

The dimensions are 2 m, 1 m and 4 m as shown.

What volume of sand is in the lorry?

G3 Another lorry full of sand has dimensions 1.9 m, 1.1 m and 4.2 m. What is the volume of sand?

G4 A large paddling pool has the following dimensions:

length = 6 m
width = 3 m
depth = 0.3 m.

Find the number of cubic metres of water needed to fill the pool.

G5 Another paddling pool has dimensions:

length = 5.5 m
width = 2.5 m
depth = 25 cm.

Find the number of cubic metres of water needed to fill the pool, but take care – all three dimensions must be in metres before you multiply.

UNIT 2 Angles

A Rotation

You have already met some shapes with **rotational symmetry**.

A square, for example, when rotated about its centre will fit exactly over its original position in four ways. This is called rotational symmetry of order 4.

So a square will look the same when rotated through a quarter turn.

A quarter turn is so common that it has a special name – a **right angle**.

A right angle is one quarter of a complete turn.

If you face north and make a quarter turn to the east, you have turned through a right angle.

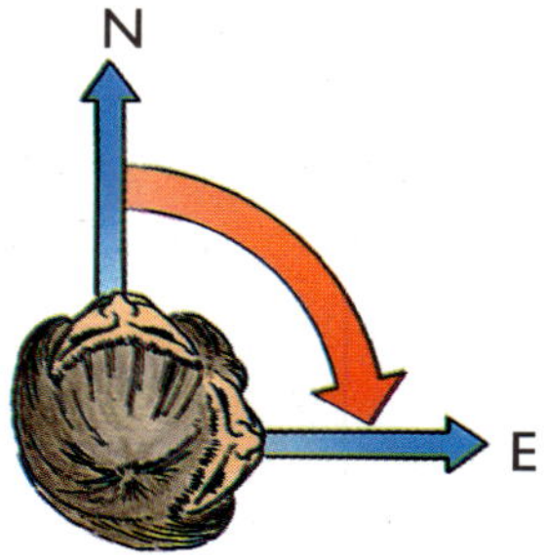

A1 If you face south and make a half turn, what direction do you face?

If you have used LOGO, `rt 90` makes a quarter turn to the right. That is, the turtle turns through a right angle.

Imagine that you are holding a stick straight out in front of you.

Make a quarter turn to the right.

A right angle is indicated by the positions of the arms at the beginning and end of the turn.

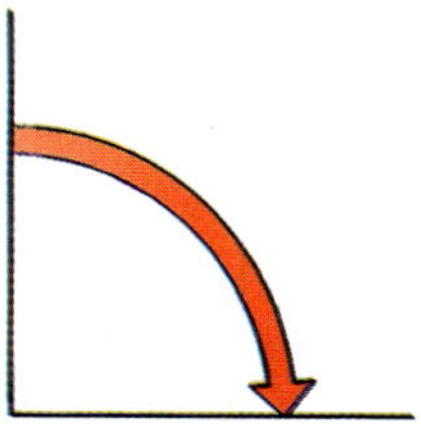

You will notice that the corners of rooms, windows and furniture are usually right angles.

A2 List six different right angles in the room.

Remember that a right angle does not depend on the length of its 'arms'

or its position.

The important idea is that to move from one arm to the other, you make a quarter turn or right angle.

In the next section you will look at different sizes of angle, but the same idea of rotation from one arm to the other is still true.

When you cut a circular (or round) cake, you make your first cut to the centre.

Then you move the knife, or **rotate** it, about the centre of the cake, to a new position and make a second cut.

You can rotate the knife to the left or the right.

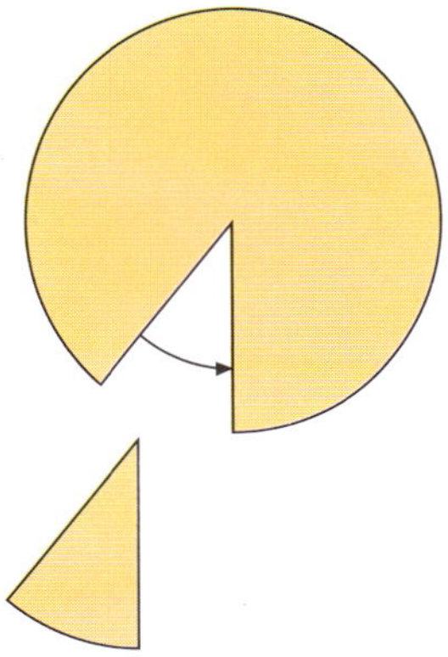

The two cuts are the **arms** of an **angle**.

B A piece of cake

Aunt Mary is offering a cake to her niece Anne.

If you were visiting your aunt which piece would you take?

The largest, the smallest, or another piece? Why?

Here are the pieces of cake.

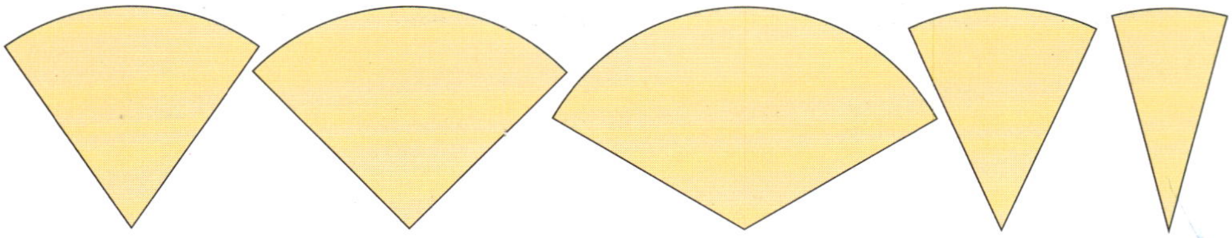

B1 Which is the largest piece of cake?

B2 Which is the smallest piece of cake?

B3 How did you decide which is the largest and which is the smallest? (One method is to look at the size of the angles and compare them.)

B4 Which piece of cake has an angle the size of a right angle?

B5 List the five pieces of cake in order of size from the smallest to largest.

B6 How many pieces of cake have an **acute** angle (less than 90°)?

B7 How many pieces of cake have **obtuse** angles (between 90° and 180°)?

Measuring angles

angle measurer

You will need an angle measurer.

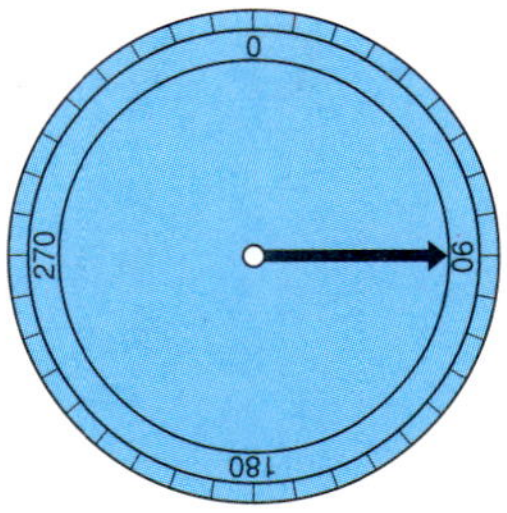

Look at the angle measurer on the right.

It shows that if you turn through a whole circle you turn 360°. The pointer is showing 90°.

To measure an angle accurately, you must:

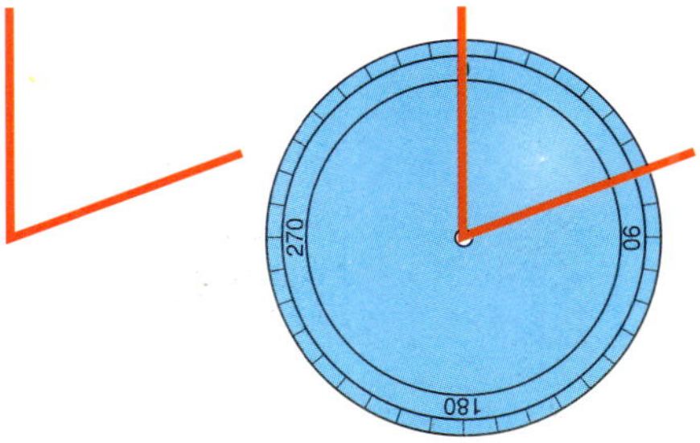

- **put the centre of the angle indicator over the corner of the angle**
- **and the 0° over one of the arms of the angle.**

Measure the angle by turning the pointer through the angle as shown. (Check: is it 70° or 290°?)

B8 Check that the first piece of cake **a** has an angle of 70°.

B9 Now measure the angles of the other four pieces of cake.

B10 Measure these angles as accurately as you can.

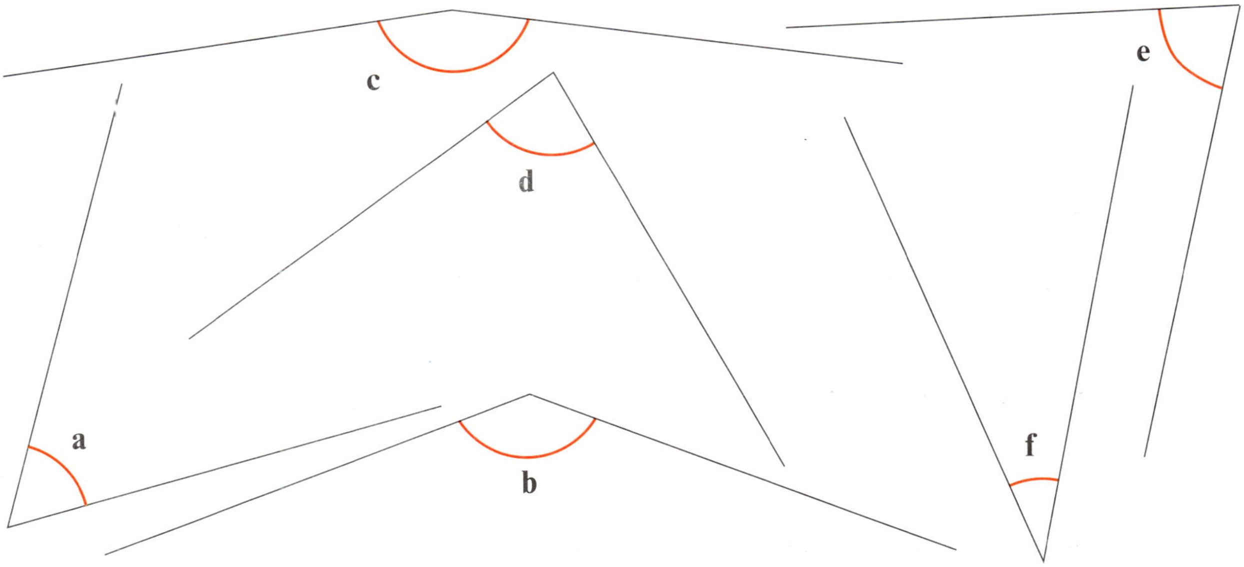

B11 Write down any four of these angles that you can put together to form a complete turn.

C Drawing angles

angle measurer

You will need an angle measurer and compasses.

C1 Draw a circle of radius 5 cm.

C2 Draw in one radius as shown.

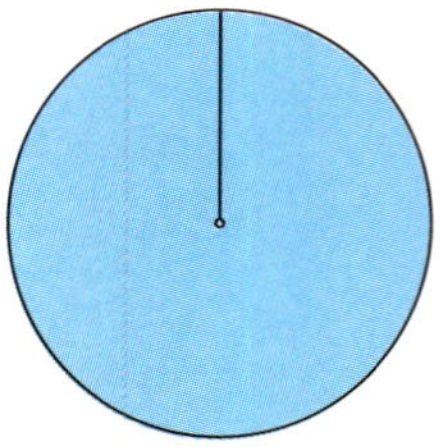

C3 Measure an angle of 70° at the centre.
Draw a line.

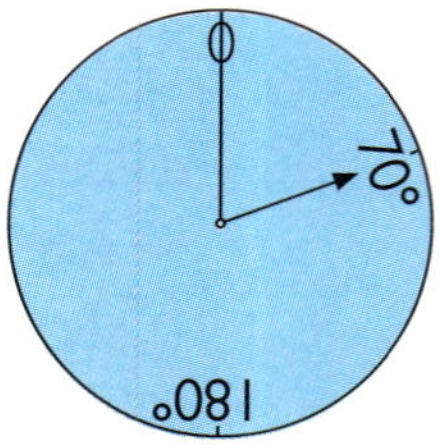

C4 Use this new line to measure an angle of 30°.

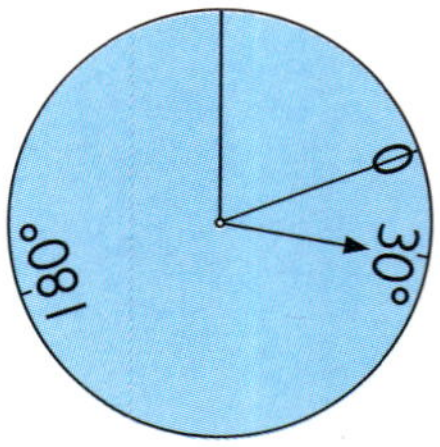

C5 Continue in the same way drawing angles of 120°, 90° and 50°.

If all your angles do not fit exactly then check your measurements.

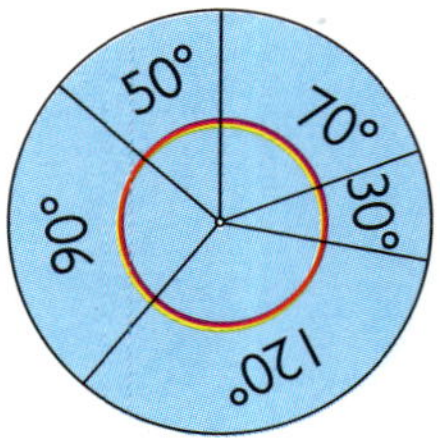

Cake cutting

C6 On a piece of paper, draw six circles of radius 5 cm.
Each circle represents a cake.

Cut the first cake into 3 equal pieces.
All three angles add up to 360°.
Each angle is 360° ÷ 3 = 120°.

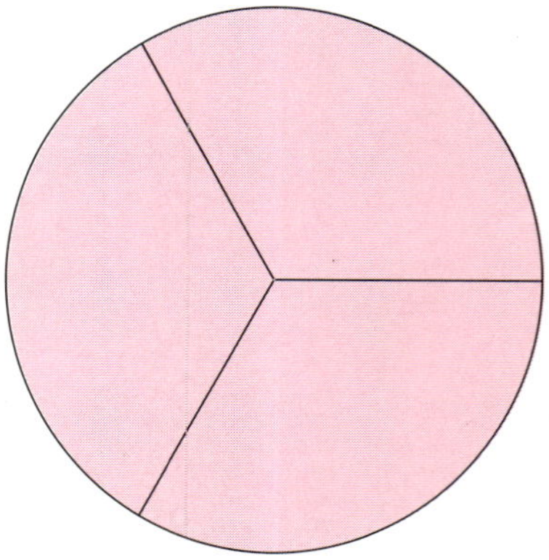

Cut the second cake into 4 equal pieces.

Cut the remaining cakes into 5, 6, 8 and 10 equal pieces.

C7 Copy and complete this table for the six cakes:

Cake	Number of pieces	Size of each piece
1	3	360° ÷ 3 = 120°
2	4	360° ÷ 4 =
3	5	
4	6	
5	8	
6	10	

You should have noticed that:

Angles that meet at a point add up to 360°.

For example, to find angle x:

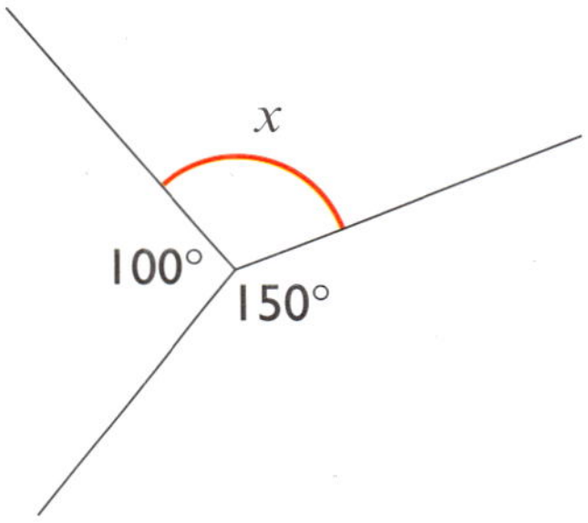

The angles 100°, 150° and x must add up to 360°.
$100° + 150° + x = 360°$,
so $x = 110°$.

C8 Without measuring, calculate the missing angles **a** to **j**. In **c** and **g**, a right angle (or 90°) is marked by two sides of a square.

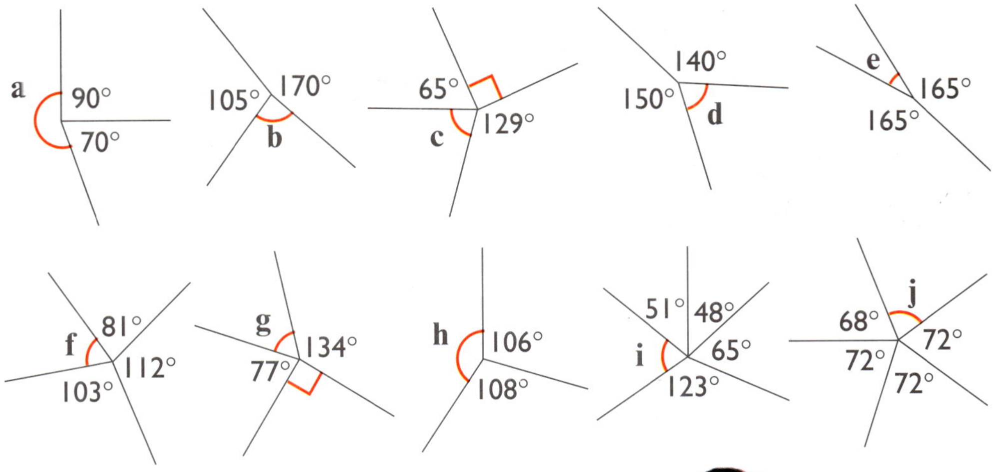

C9 **Extension work** John wants to cut a cake into four pieces so that there are two equal small pieces, one piece which is twice as big and one which is four times as big as each of the small pieces.

D Half-moon cakes

A half-moon cake is in the shape of a semicircle.

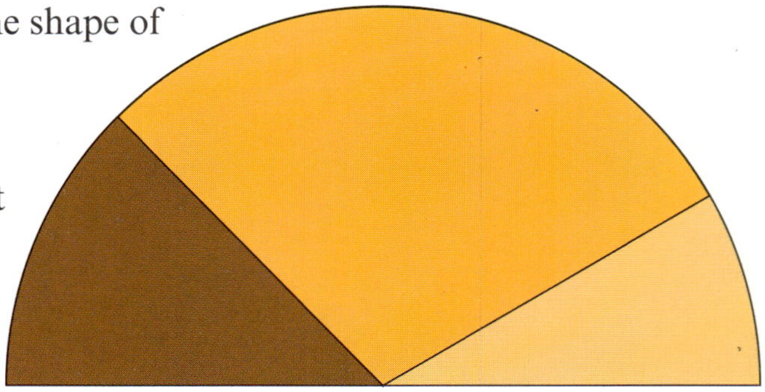

D1 If a half-moon cake is cut into three unequal pieces what is the sum (adding together) of the angles of all three pieces?

D2 How many 60° angle-sized pieces can you cut from a half-moon cake?

This shows us that:

Angles on a straight line add up to 180°.

We can use this fact to calculate angles.

For example, to find angle x:

$x = 180° - (90° + 36°)$
$x = 180° - 126°$
$x = 54°$

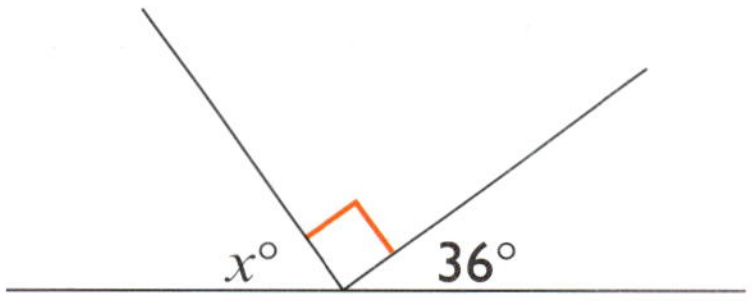

D3 Calculate the size of the missing angles **a** to **l**.

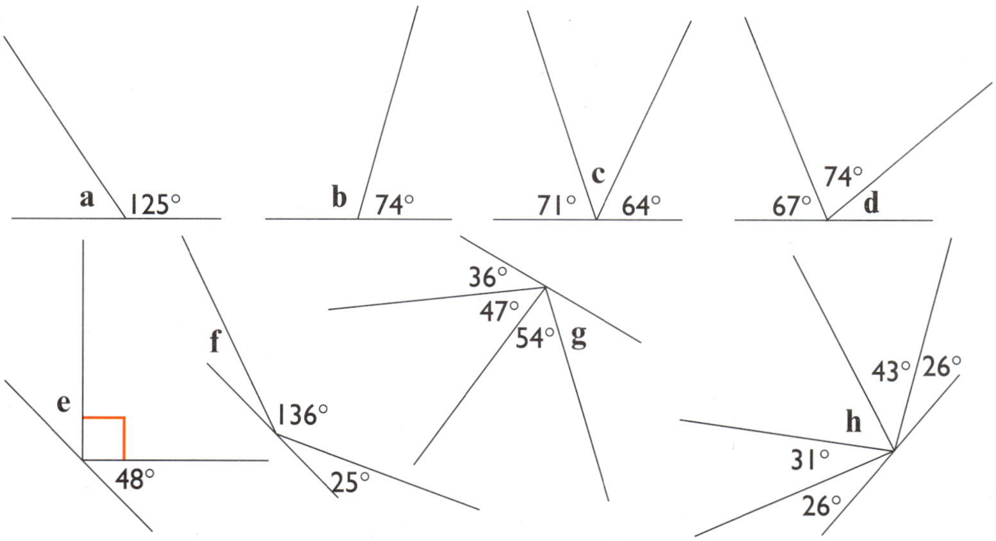

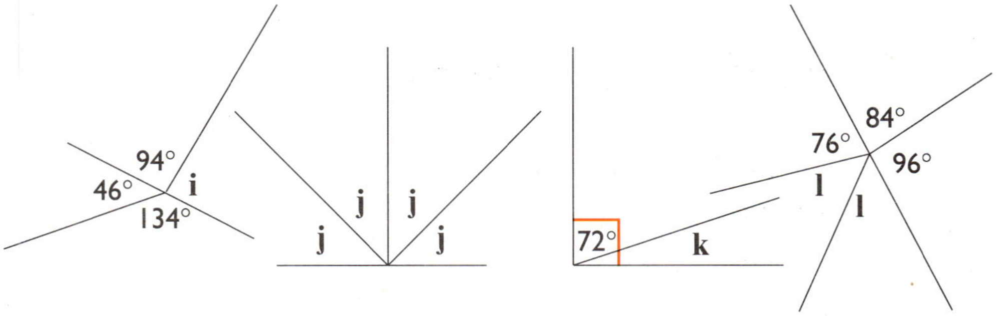

D4 Draw an angle of 53°.

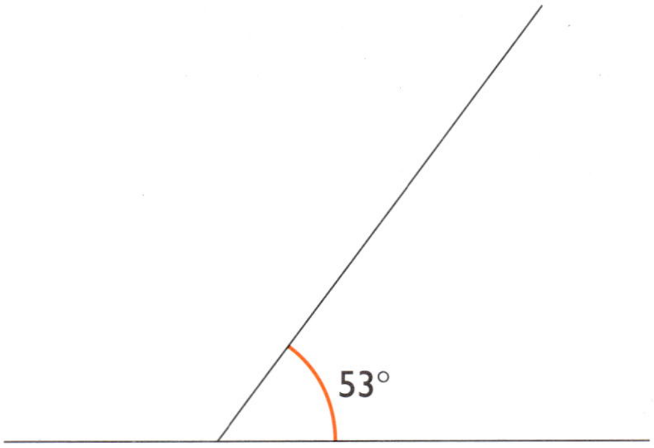

Extend one of the arms of the angle, as shown, to make an obtuse angle.

Measure the obtuse angle. Do you get exactly 127°?

How far out from 127° would you count as correct?

D5 Draw an angle of 136°.

Extend one of the arms of the angle to make an acute angle.

Measure the angle and add your result to 136°. Do you get 180°?

D6 Draw three angles of 45°, 50° and 34° as shown:

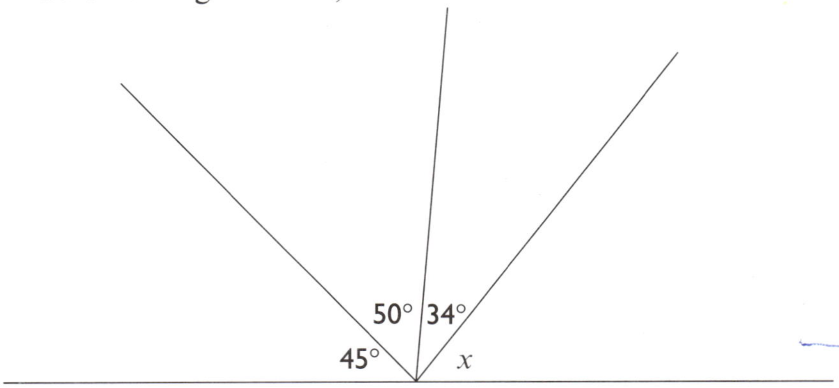

Measure *and* calculate the angle x.

E Triangles

scissors
scrap paper

You will need scissors and scrap paper.

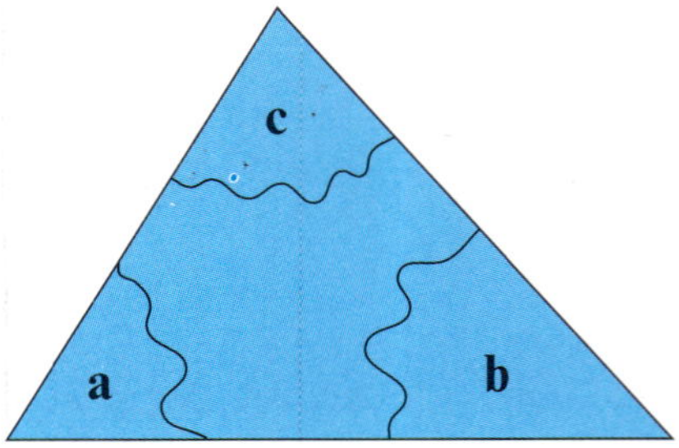

E1 **a** Draw a triangle on scrap paper.

b Cut out the triangle.

c Tear off each corner.

d Place the three angles (corners) together.

e What do you notice?

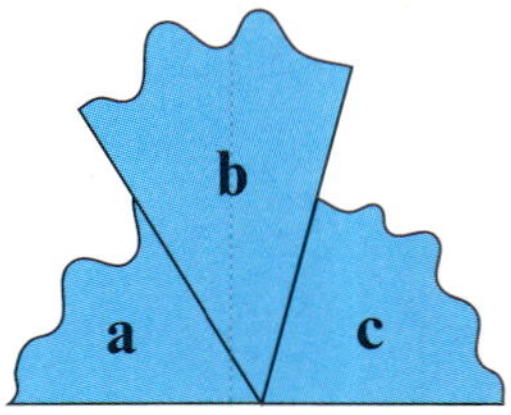

E2 Repeat with a different triangle.

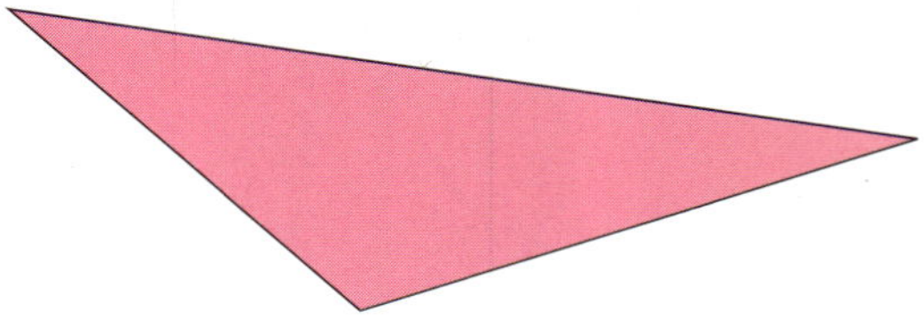

You should have noticed that:

The three angles of a triangle add up to 180°.

E3 Use the fact that the sum of the angles of a triangle is 180° to calculate the values of angles **a** to **h**.

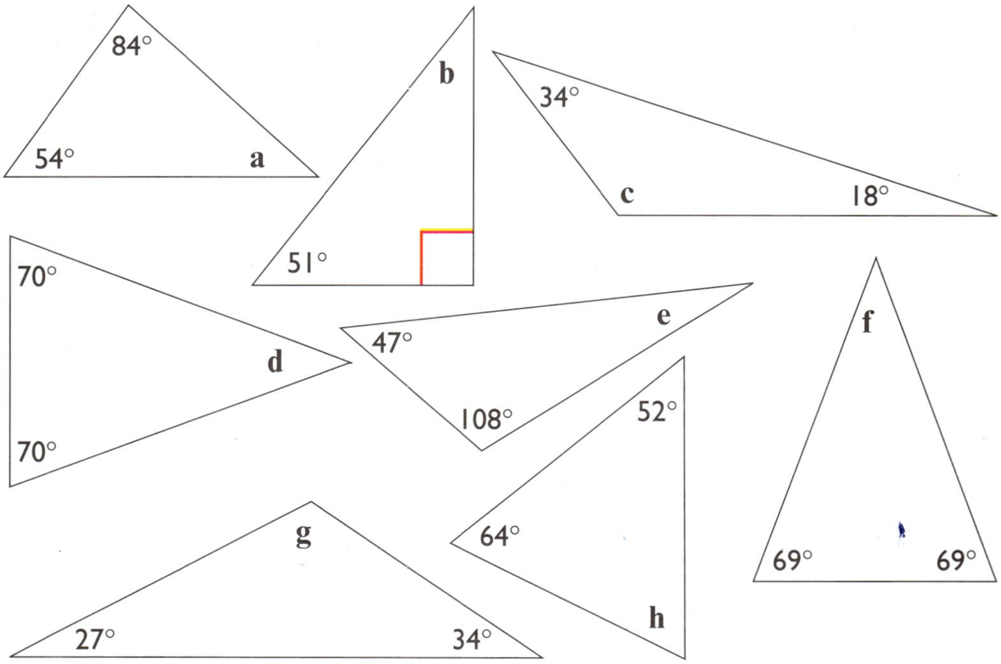

A triangle with all three sides equal is called **equilateral**.

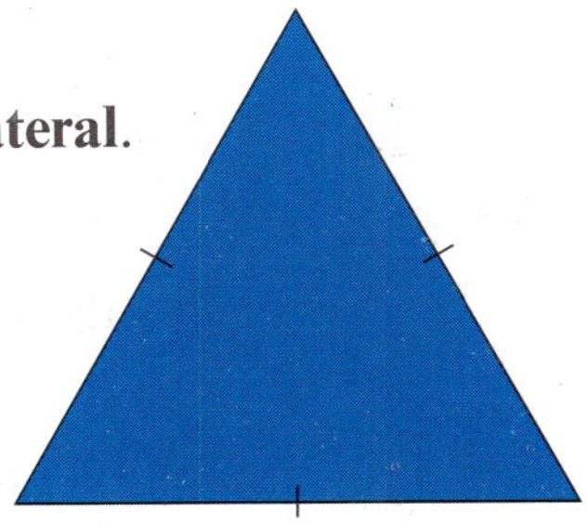

E4 In an equilateral triangle, all the angles are equal. What is the size of each angle?

E5 **a** What is the order of rotational symmetry of an equilateral triangle?

b How many mirror lines of symmetry has an equilateral triangle?

A triangle with two sides equal is called **isosceles**.

E6 Angles **d**, **f** and **h** of question **E3** are each in isosceles triangles.

How can you tell that the triangles are isosceles?

Isosceles means 'equal legs' or equal sides.

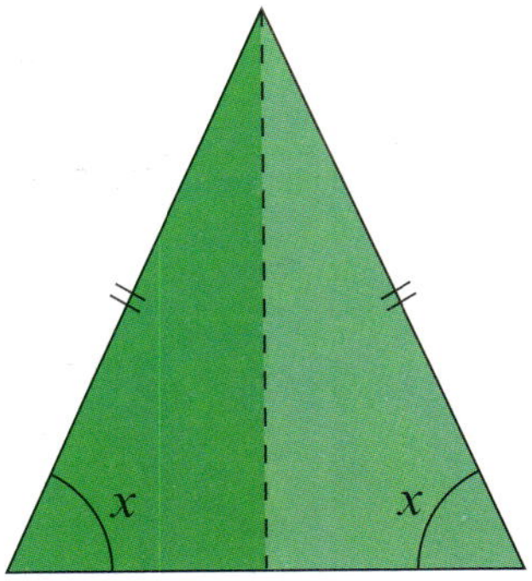

By looking at the mirror symmetry about the dotted line, it is clear that the 'base angles', marked x, are equal.

If one angle of an isosceles triangle is known, it is possible to calculate the other two angles.

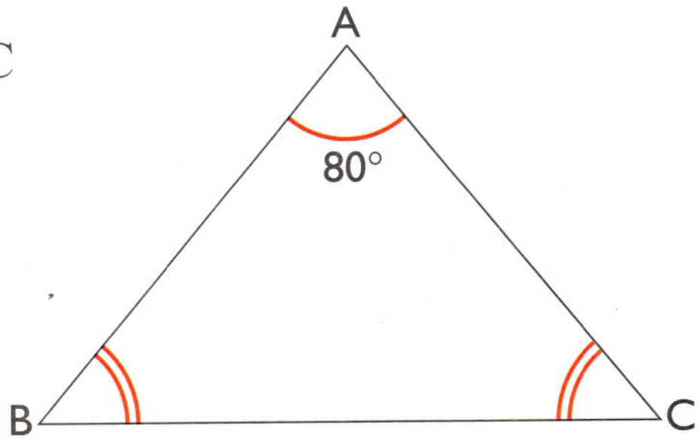

For example, in triangle ABC, AB = AC and the angle at A is 80°.

The base angles are equal.
As A is 80°, the base angles must add up to 100°, so each base angle is 50°.

E7 Calculate the base angles of isosceles triangle DEF in which DE = DF and angle D = 90°.

E8 If one of the base angles of an isosceles triangle is 35°, write down the values of the other two angles.

UNIT 3 Circles

A Circles around us

A circle is one of the commonest shapes around:

We see circles in wheels, in mugs, in tops of cans and bottles and many more things.

A1 Make a list of six circles in the room.

A2 Does the size of a circle make a difference to its shape?

A3 Describe the rotational symmetry of a circle.

A4 How many mirror lines of symmetry can you find on a circle?

In answering questions **A3** and **A4**, you will have found that a circle is very symmetrical. It is the most symmetrical shape.

If you rotate a circle about its centre, it always looks the same. It does not matter whether you turn it 1° or 45° or 180°.

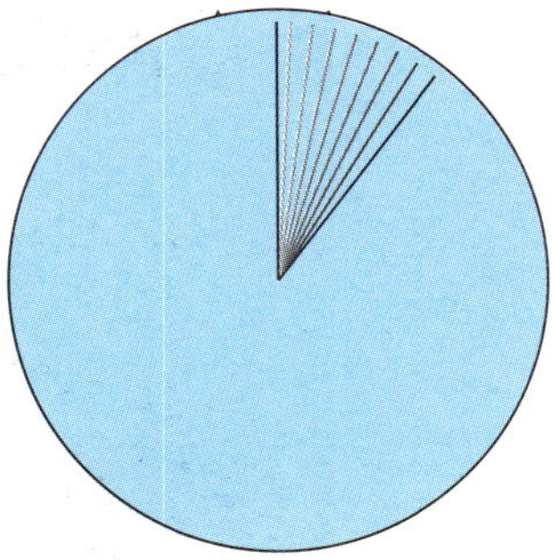

It has as many different orders of rotational symmetry as you wish. We sometimes say that the order of rotational symmetry of a circle is infinite.

Similarly, a circle has an infinity of mirror lines of symmetry. Any line which passes through the centre of a circle, called a diameter, is a line of symmetry.

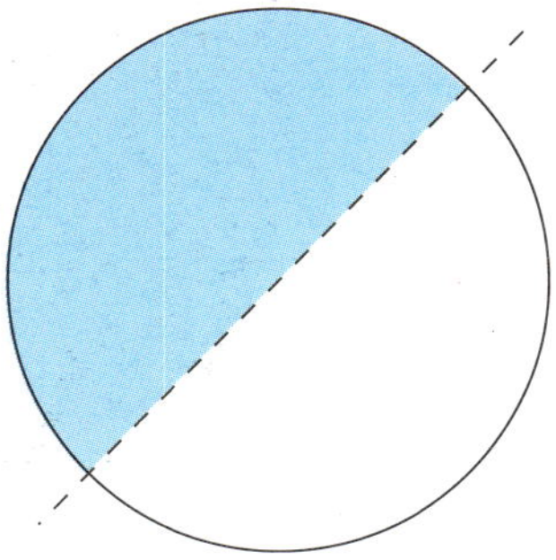

Another way of looking at it is to think of folding a circle along a diameter. It always folds exactly on to itself whichever diameter you choose.

A5 Look at a circle in the room. How can you be certain that it is a circle? Do you need to know that all its diameters are the same length?

Usually, when you look at a circular object, you know it has a circle even though you may see an oval shape called an ellipse.

A6 Look at the pictures on the opposite page.

Write down those items where the picture really is a circle (or very close to a circle) and those where you see an ellipse.

B Shortest route

Which is the shorter route to the Drive-In?
Who will get there first depends on their speeds. Why?

The car will need to drive around the roundabout.
That is, half way round the circle, or half the **circumference**.

The woman will have to walk across the centre of the roundabout.
The footpath is the **diameter** of the circle.

The woman who is walking along the diameter of the circle has the shorter route as this is a straight line.

B1 Write down two reasons why the woman might get to the Drive-In first.

B2 Write down two reasons why the car might get to the Drive-In first.

The woman has to walk the diameter of the circle. If she was at the centre, then she would need to walk only half of the diameter.
This is known as the **radius**.

The diagram shows a circle.

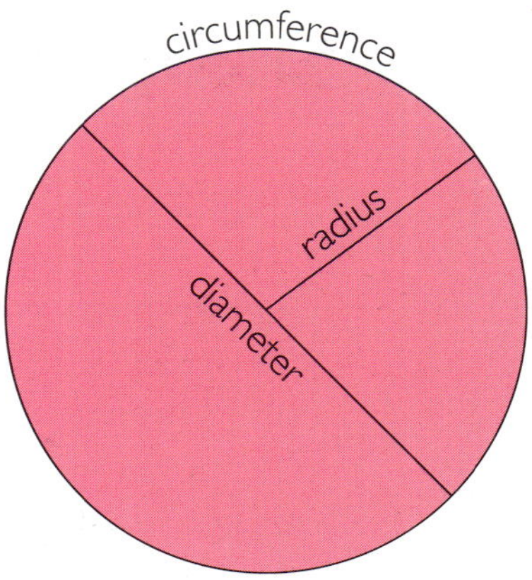

B3 Copy and complete these sentences:

a The circumference of a circle is…

b The diameter of a circle is …

c The radius of a circle is …

Pounds, shillings and pence

These are some of the coins used before 1971 when the currency in the United Kingdom was decimalized.

B4 Copy the table. Measure each coin. Write down its diameter and radius. (The two shillings coin was known as a florin.)

	Diameter	Radius	Value in decimal coins
Halfcrown			
Florin			
Shilling			
Sixpence			
Penny			
Halfpenny			

B5 By asking friends or relatives, or using a reference book, write in the value for each coin in present money.

B6 **a** Look at the results in your table. Large coins are not always worth more than small coins. Give some examples.

b Make a statement about the value and size of all the coins.

B7 Are all present coins circles? It is possible to draw all of the present coins with a pair of compasses. Try drawing a 50p piece.

C Using compasses

coloured pencils

You will need a pair of compasses, a pencil, a ruler and coloured pencils.

This six-petal flower was drawn using compasses set to a radius of 4 cm.

4cm flower

Why do you think this is called a 4 cm flower?

C1 Open your compasses to a radius of 3 cm. Draw a 3 cm flower and colour in your pattern.

C2 Draw a flower like the one shown here. You will need to draw the larger circle with radius 5 cm and the smaller one with radius 2 cm.

C3 How much greater is the diameter of the larger circle than that of the smaller circle?

C4 What is the order of rotational symmetry of the flower in question **C2**?

The six-pointed star

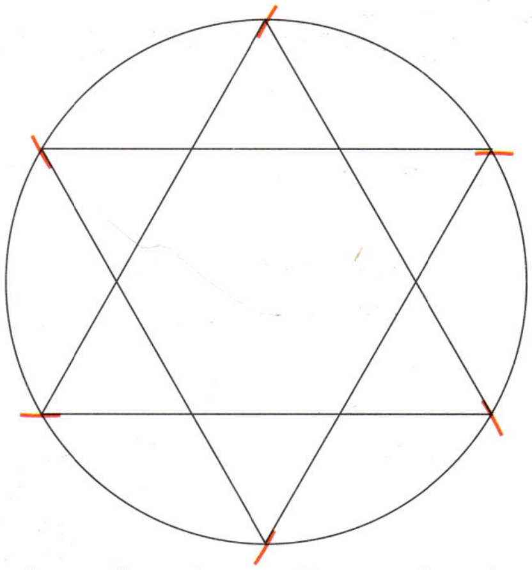

C5 How many triangles make a six-pointed star?

C6 Using a radius of 4 cm construct a six-pointed star. Draw the circle first and then, keeping the same radius, mark six points round the circle.

Look at your star. How many crossovers (intersections) are there? How many straight lines? How many regions?

The Olympic investigation

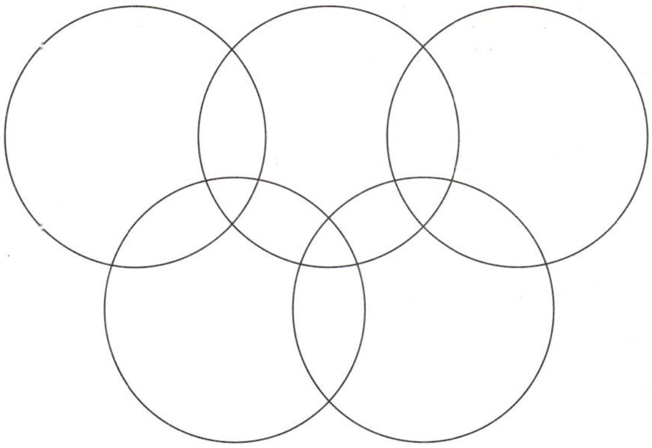

C7 How many crossovers are there in each diagram?

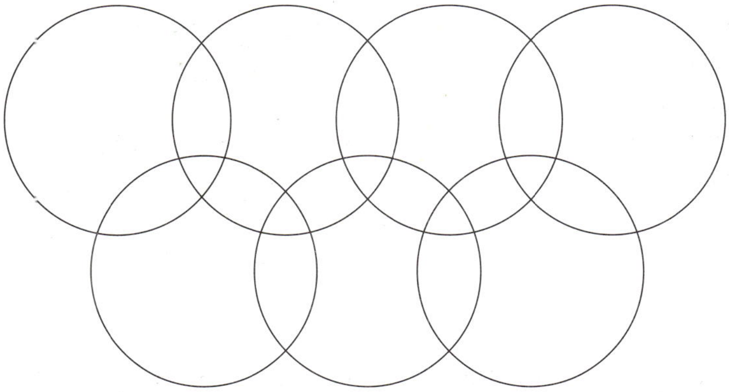

C8 How many crossovers are there with seven circles? Investigate for other sized overlapping diagrams. How many crossovers for 19 circles? Describe any patterns you can see.

D The circumference

cylindrical objects
scissors

You will need a number of cylindrical objects and scissors.

Make some 1 cm wide strips about 30 cm long by cutting up 1cm squared paper. You will find this section easier if you work with a neighbour to measure each of your cylinders.

D1 Draw a table like the one shown below.

Object	Diameter	Circumference
soup can	7 cm	22 cm

D2 In the first column, list the circular objects you have collected. Measure each diameter and write it in the second column.

To measure the circumference of a tin, take a strip of centimetre paper and wrap it round like this:

Mark the strip and check it is the correct length by measuring again.

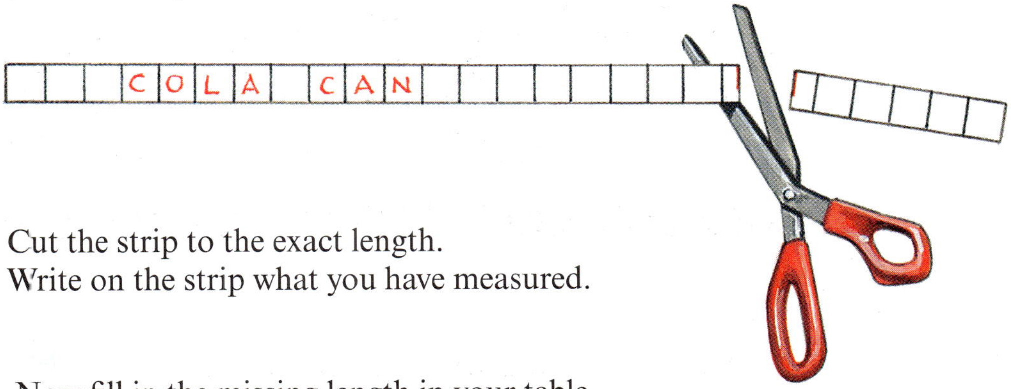

Cut the strip to the exact length.
Write on the strip what you have measured.

D3 Now fill in the missing length in your table.

D4 Measure the circumference for each of your other cylinders and complete the table. Remember to label and keep each strip.

D5 Look at your completed table.

a Find the object with the largest diameter.
What do you notice about its circumference?

b Find the object with the smallest diameter.
What do you notice about its circumference?

D6 In your table, is the circumference of each object always longer than the diameter? About how many times longer than the diameter is the circumference?

E Round up

You have learnt three important parts of the circle:

- The **diameter** – the distance across the circle through the centre
- The **radius** – half the diameter and the distance that you use to draw a circle with compasses
- The **circumference** – the distance round the circle or its perimeter.

E1 Measure the radius and diameter of this circle:

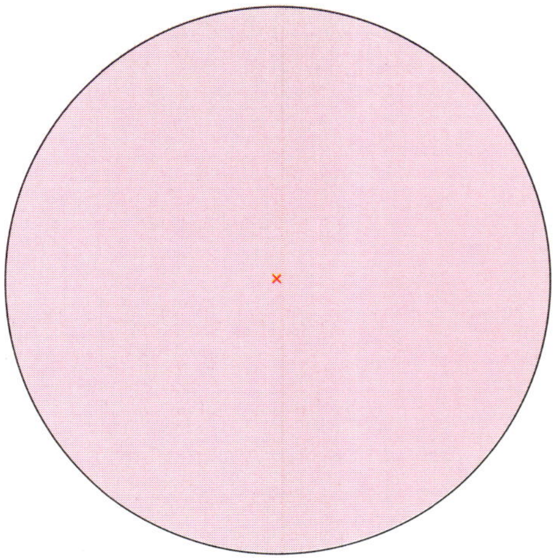

E2 A circle has a diameter of 10 centimetres. What is its radius?

E3 What is the diameter of a circle with radius 2.5 cm?

E4

A chalk mark is put on a tyre and on the ground.

The wheel is rolled along the ground in a straight line until the chalk mark on the tyre touches the ground again. A second mark is made on the ground.

Is the distance between the two marks on the ground the same as the circumference of the circle?

E5 Look at the table you completed in Section D.

Repeat the measurement of the circumference of one of the objects by rolling it along a ruler until a mark on the rim is on the ruler again.

Did you get the same answer as before?
Which is the more accurate way of measuring the circumference?

E6 Find two round objects with the diameter of one double the diameter of the other.

When you roll them along a ruler, is the circumference of one double the circumference of the other?

E7 How would you measure the diameter of the trunk of a very large tree?

UNIT 4 All about boxes

A Boxes

Have you noticed how many boxes we use every day?

They come in a variety of shapes and sizes.

A1 Name the boxes in the picture which have the shape of:

a a cuboid **b** a triangular prism

c an hexagonal prism **d** a cylinder.

Making an Oxo box

An Oxo box is a cuboid which holds twelve Oxo cubes.

The box is made from a piece of card shaped like a rectangle.

A flat net for the box is pressed out from the sheet of card.

It is then folded and glued in the shape of the Oxo box.

If the box is opened out, we get the net on the opposite page.

S2:2

A2 Use Worksheet S2:2 or make a copy of the net opposite.

Carefully cut it out and score along the dotted lines to make sharp edges. Stick down the flaps. Remember the lid should open!

A3 Using squared paper, design the net of an Oxo cube box to hold eight cubes.

The length of each side of an Oxo cube is 2 cm.

Before you draw out the net accurately, you will need to sketch your design, writing in all the measurements.

Inside bigger boxes

The three Oxo boxes shown here hold 4, 6 and 12 cubes as shown.

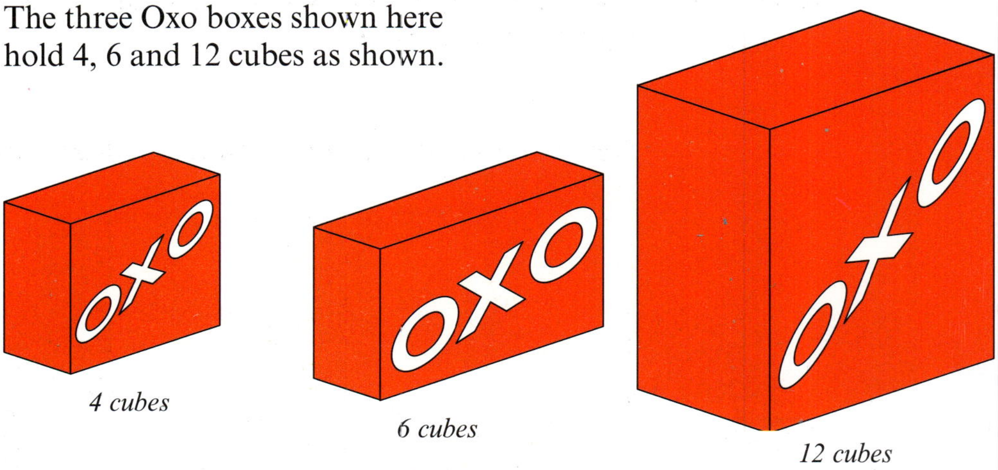

Inside the smallest box there are 4 cubes like this:

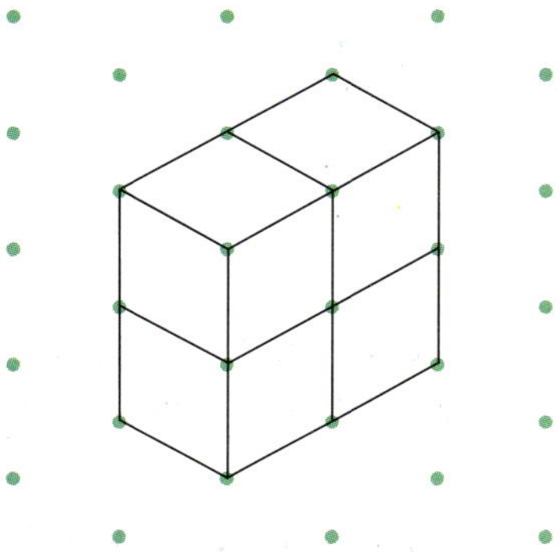

dotty triangle paper

A4 Use dotty triangle paper to copy this diagram.

A5 Use dotty triangle paper to draw the Oxo cubes inside:

a the 6 pack

b the 12 pack.

A6 One Oxo cube is shown here next to the box designed to hold 6 cubes.

If the length of each side of an Oxo cube is 2 cm, find the width, length and height of the Oxo box. (The Oxo cubes are packed tightly inside.)

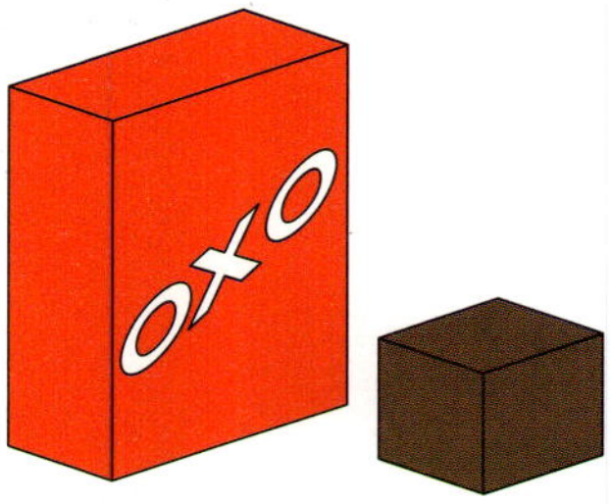

Cubes

An Oxo cube is an example of a cube.

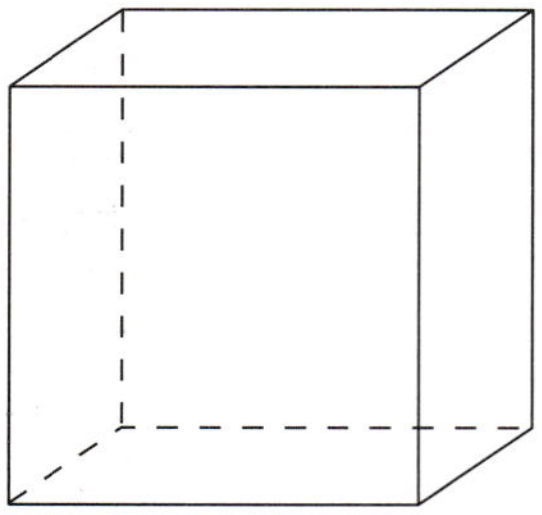

A7 **a** How many faces has a cube?

b How many edges has a cube?

c How many corners (vertices) has a cube?

Each of the nets below is made from 6 squares.
You may remember that they are known as hexominoes and that some of them can be folded to make a cube.

A8 Look at these hexominoes and write down which of them make cubes.

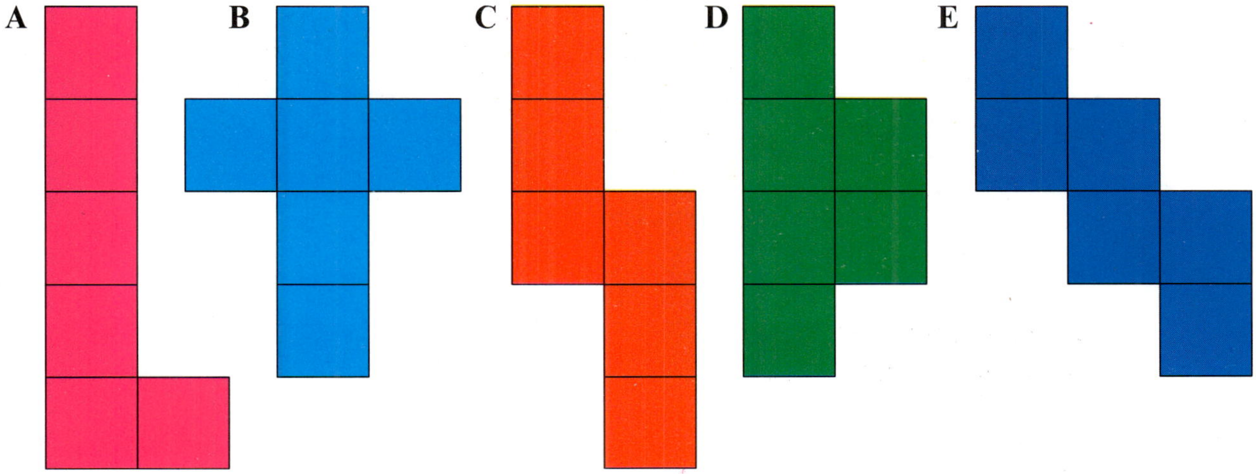

dotty square paper

A9 On dotty square paper, make nets of your own for three different hexominoes which will fold to make a cube.

A 1 cm cube has six faces, each of which has area 1 cm^2.
That is, the total surface area of a 1cm cube is 6 cm^2.

A10 Look at this 2 cm cube:

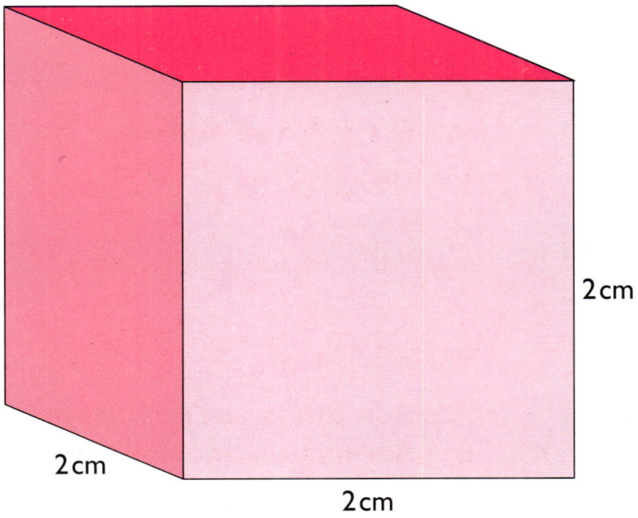

a What area in cm^2 of card would you need to make one face of this 2 cm cube?

b On dotty square paper, make a net for this 2 cm cube.

c What is the total surface area of this cube?

d How many small 1 cm cubes will fit into the 2 cm cube?

B Prisms and polyhedra

B1 This is a picture of a triangular prism.

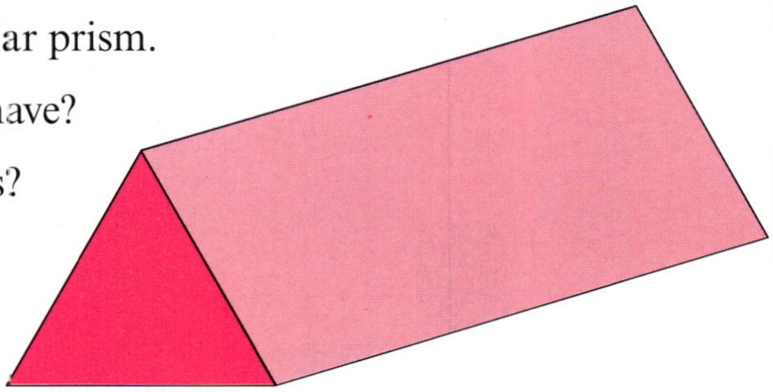

a How many faces does it have?

b What shapes are the faces?

c Does it have rotational symmetry?

Here is the net of a triangular prism:

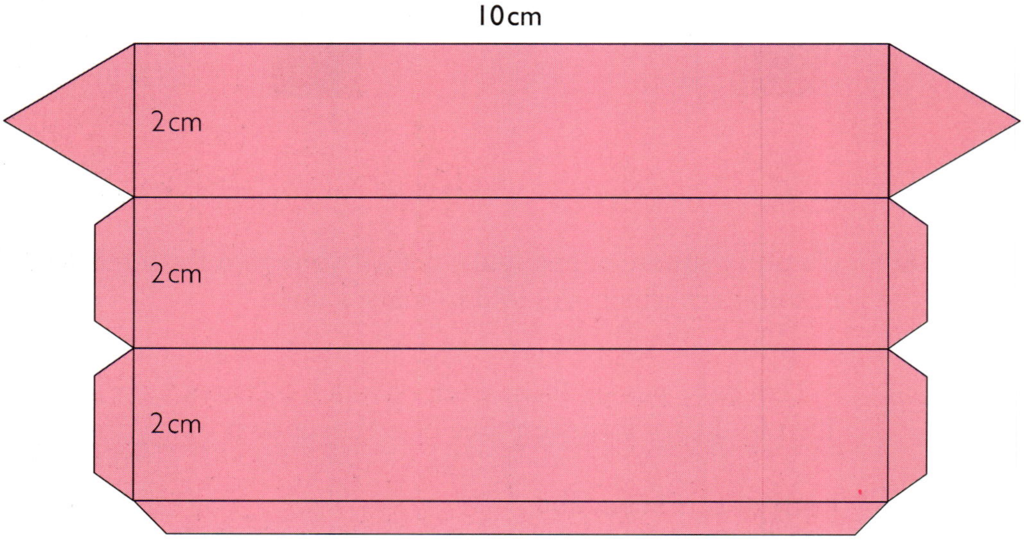

B2 If each of the rectangular faces of the triangular prism is 10 cm × 2 cm:

a what is special about the triangle that forms the end of the prism?

b what name do we give this triangle?

B3 Copy the net on to dotty square paper and make the prism.

Polyhedra

A **polyhedron** is a solid shape, such as a cube, with many faces. The name polyhedron comes from the Greek 'polys' meaning 'many' and 'hedra' meaning seat or side. The plural is **polyhedra**.

Euler's formula

Euler was a famous and creative eighteenth-century Swiss mathematician. He spent much time investigating solids and polyhedra. In 1752 he rediscovered a relationship which had been used as early as 1640 by the French mathematician Descartes. The relationship connects the number of faces, edges and vertices (corners) of polyhedra which you will now rediscover.

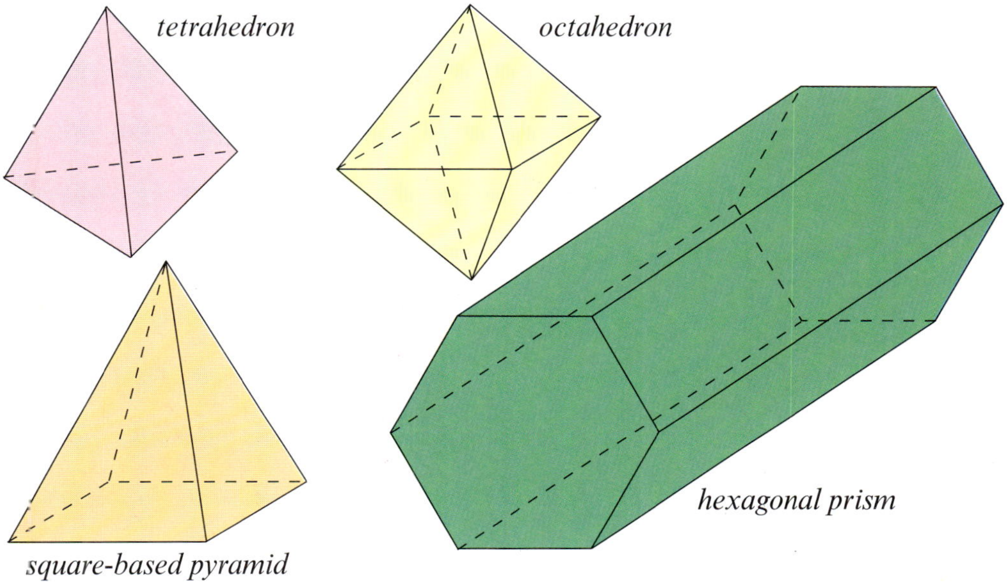

S2:3

B4 Copy and complete this table or use Worksheet S2:3.

Name of polyhedron	Number of faces, *F*	Number of vertices, *V*	Number of edges, *E*
cube	6		
triangular prism		6	
hexagonal prism			18
tetrahedron			
square-based pyramid			
octahedron			

B5 Euler's formula or relationship connects F, V and E.
See if you can find it. (Hint: compare $F + V$ with E.)

Now try another familiar solid, such as a cuboid, to see if Euler's formula works. It should. $F + V - E = 2$ is true for all polyhedra.

C Irregular boxes

Many boxes we use are not regular.
That is, they look different as they are turned round.
Here is a net for a very well-known box.

C1 What does this box contain? (Do you recognize it?)

C2 How many faces does it have?

C3 What do we call the shape used for the side of the box?

C4 What is the shape of the lid?
Do the four flaps at the bottom fold to give the same shape?

C5 Make a copy of the net and use it to make the box.

C6 Check that Euler's formula works for this polyhedron too.

D Mental shapes – using your imagination

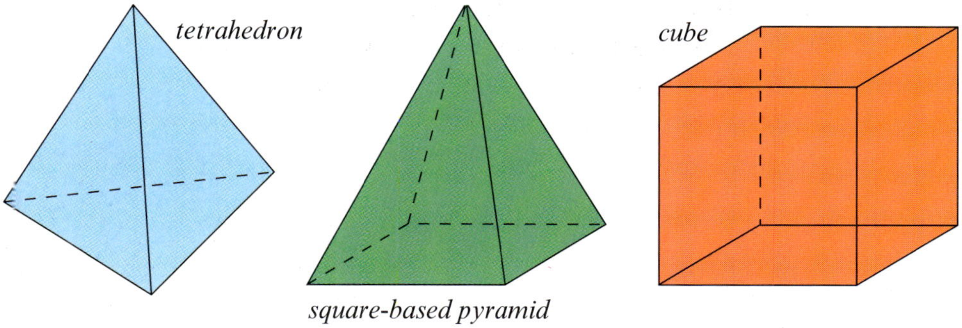

D1 Imagine that you have two identical cubes.

Place them together with a square face exactly on a square face.

a How many faces does the new solid have?

b How many edges does the new solid have?

c How many vertices are there?

D2 Now imagine you have two identical square-based pyramids. Put the square bases together.

a How many faces edges and vertices are there on the new solid?

b What is the name of the new polyhedron?

D3 Suppose you have a cube in one hand and a square-based pyramid in the other.

Suppose you put the square face of the pyramid against one of the square faces of the cube, which is identical in size. Imagine the new solid.

How many faces, edges and vertices does it have?

D4 This time you have a tetrahedron and a square-based pyramid whose triangular faces are identical to those of the tetrahedron. How many faces, edges and vertices are there on this new solid?

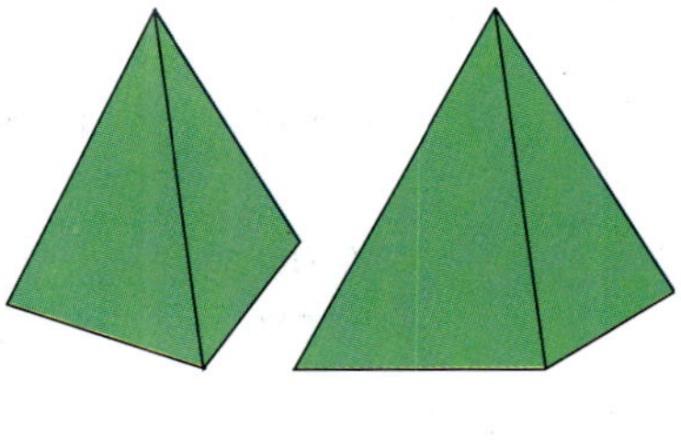

D5 **Extension work** Check all your answers by making the solids and placing them together.

E Plan views

When drawing plans for buildings, architects need to make designs which show different views of the building.

Usually there are three views: the front view (called the **front elevation**), the **side elevation** and the **plan view** (looking down from above).

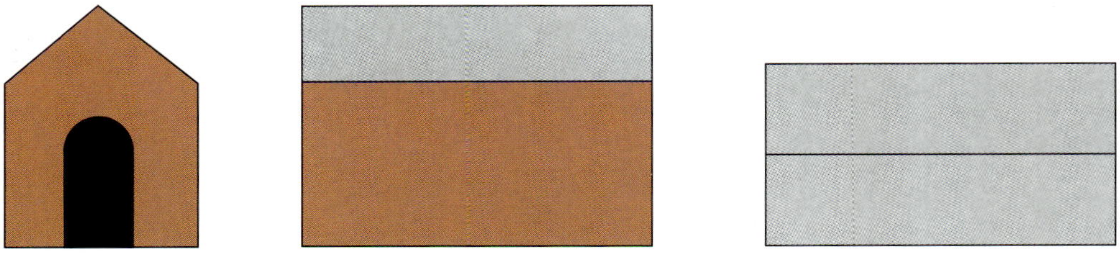

front elevation *side elevation* *plan*

E1 These three views are of the same object. What is it?

E2 You will notice that the plan view is a rectangle with an extra line.

a What does this line represent?

b How is this explained when you look at the front elevation?

E3 Here is a sketch of the object made from the three views.

Unfortunately, there is a mistake. What is it?

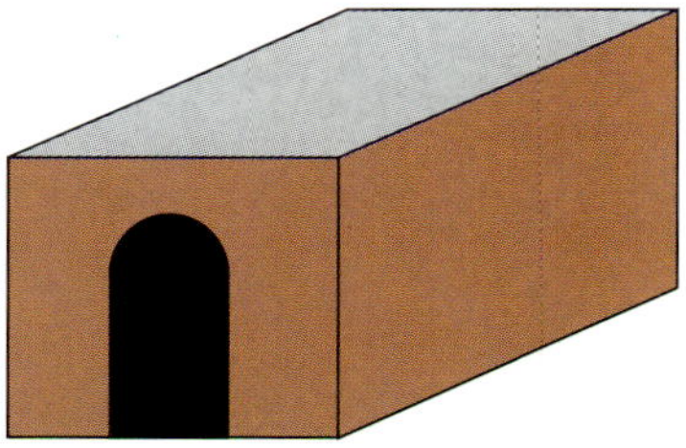

E4 Draw a sketch without making the same mistake as the artist.

E5 Some of these shapes you have already met in this Unit.
Write down the names of the solids represented by the three views given.

front elevation *side elevation* *plan*

a

b

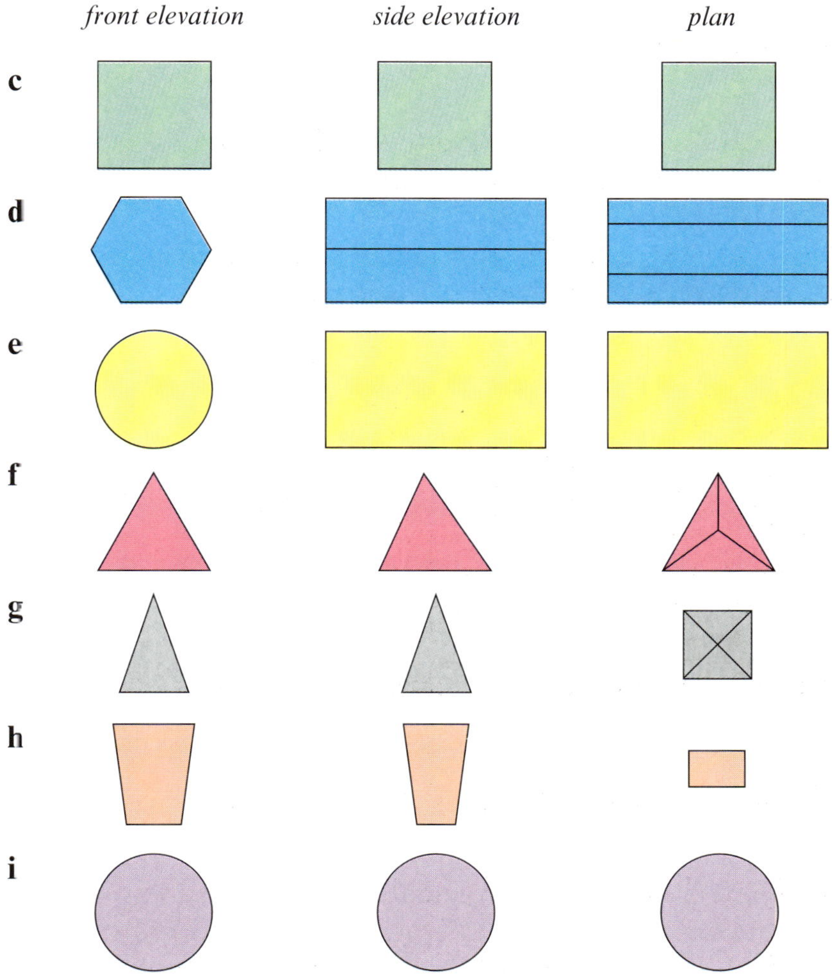

The multilink cube challenge

E6 The diagram shows four multilink cubes made in the shape of an L.

a Draw the front, side and plan views.

b Make another shape from four cubes. Draw the three views. Can a partner recognize the shape?

c Using all four multilink cubes, how many different shapes can you make so that this is one of the views?

d Make a sketch of each shape you make. Have you found the shape which has all three views the same?

UNIT 5 Construction

A Building sites

The new Tesbury's supermarket

The building of a new supermarket involves a lot of construction work, but before this can start, plans need to be drawn up. Although plans are very complex, much of the work in making them is based on quite simple geometrical constructions, particularly rectangles, triangles and parallel lines.

The land on which this supermarket was built had been a sports field. As part of the deal, Tesbury' s agreed to build a new sports complex on a new site. The new sports complex will have one rugby pitch, one football pitch, one hockey pitch and a cricket square.

These diagrams show the sizes of the pitches for the new complex. Distances are in metres.

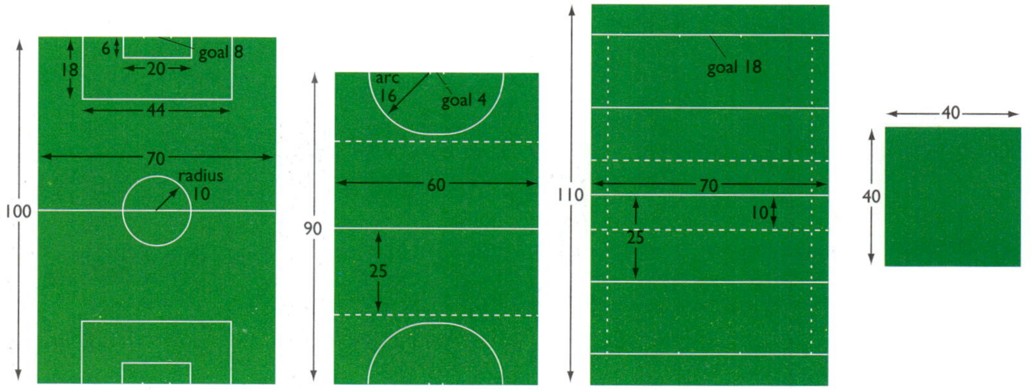

football pitch *hockey pitch* *rugby pitch* *cricket square*

A1 On squared paper (or graph paper), draw the outlines of each of these pitches accurately and cut them out carefully. Use a scale of 1 cm to 10 metres.

There will be a new clubhouse containing the changing rooms.

The diagram shows a plan of the clubhouse.

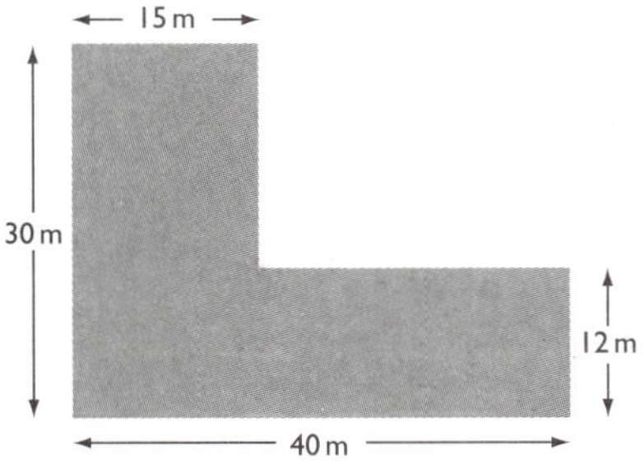

A2 Using a scale of 1 cm to 10 metres, draw and cut out the plan of the clubhouse.

The fields that are to be used for the sports ground are surrounded by a river and two roads as shown below.

The plan on the right is a smaller version of Worksheet S2:4 which is the same scale as your cut-out shapes of the pitches and clubhouse.

A3 Use Worksheet S2:4 and your cut-out shapes to plan the new sports field.

Remember that:

- the cricket square must be in the middle
- no pitches should be within 10 m of the edge of the field
- the clubhouse should be near the road and have as much car parking space as possible.

The new Tesbury's is to have a large supermarket building, a car park, a petrol station and a children's play area as shown.

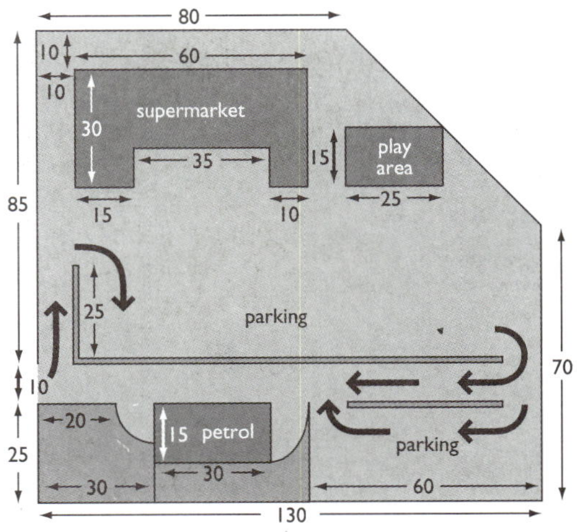

A4 On squared paper using a scale of 1 cm to 10 m, make an accurate plan of the new Tesbury's. All measurements are in metres. The arrows show the direction that cars must take.

B Constructing triangles

angle measurer

You will need a pair of compasses and an angle measurer or protractor.

Architects draw plans for buildings. They need to be able to draw all shapes accurately.

At first they may sketch the details to get an idea of the finished plan. Later, they draw their design exactly.

This requires the use of angle measurers and compasses – and a lot of practice.

Here Mike is sketching out the side view of the roof for the supermarket.

B1 You can make a scale drawing of the roof using a scale of 1 cm to 2 m.

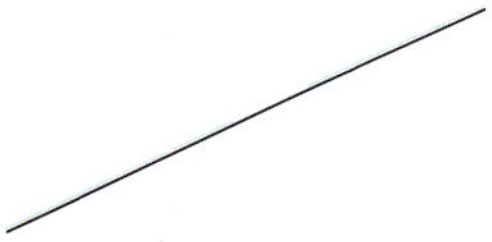

Draw a line of length 5.5 cm (11 m).

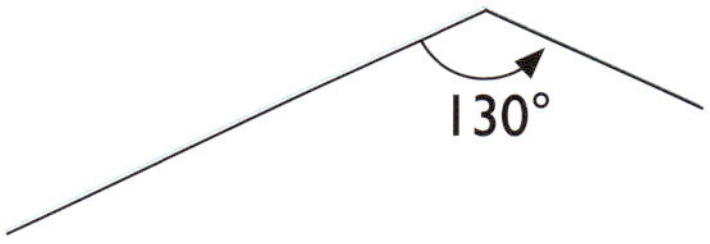

Measure an angle of 130°.

Draw in the other side of length 5.5 cm.

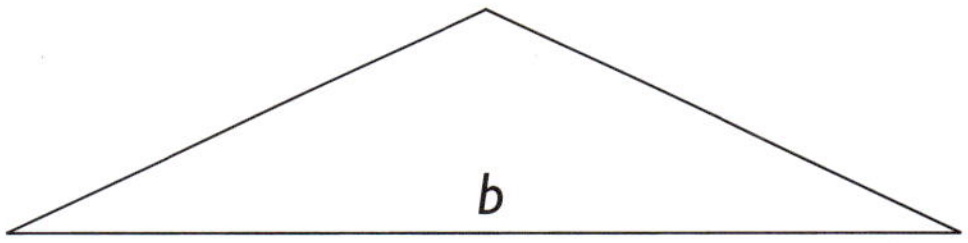

Complete the triangle.

B2 How long is the line marked *b* (the width of the supermarket at this point)? Did you get about 10 cm, making the width about 20 m?

B3 Use the same method to construct the following triangles.
Find the length of AB in metres for each question if 1 cm represents 2 m.

a

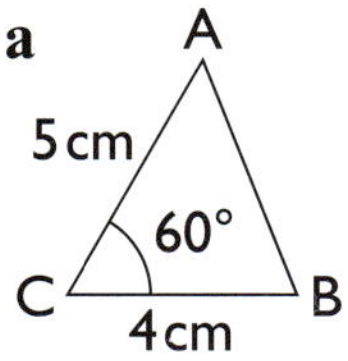

b

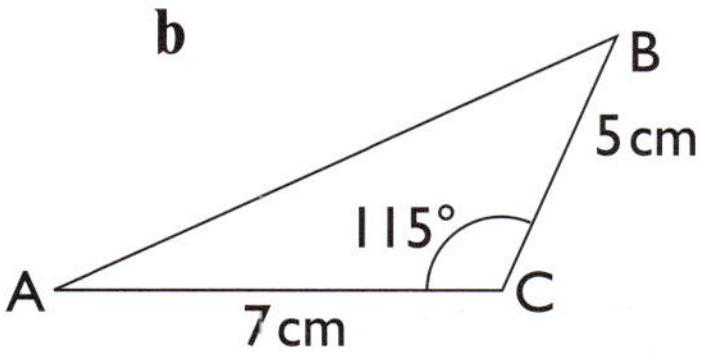

c

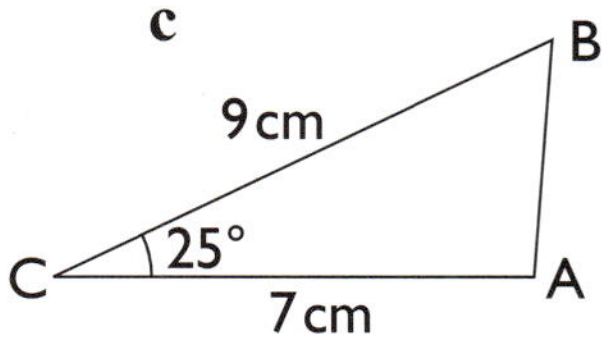

In a children's playground, the side frame for the swing is made of pieces of metal as shown.

B4 Draw the outline of the side frame accurately as follows, using a scale of 1 cm to 1 m:

a

Draw a base line of 3 cm.

b

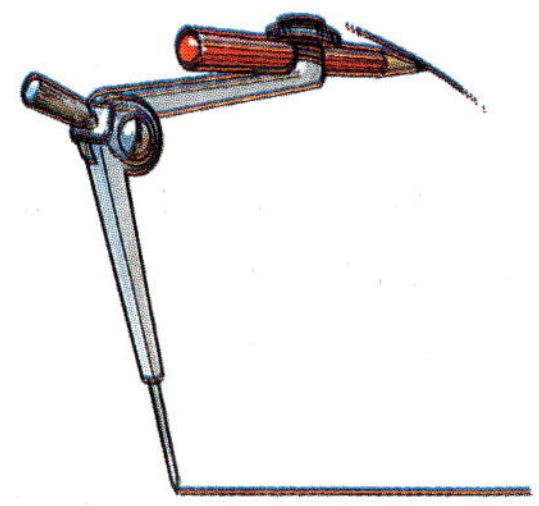

Open compasses to 4 cm and draw an arc.

c

From the other end of the base line draw another 4 cm arc.

d

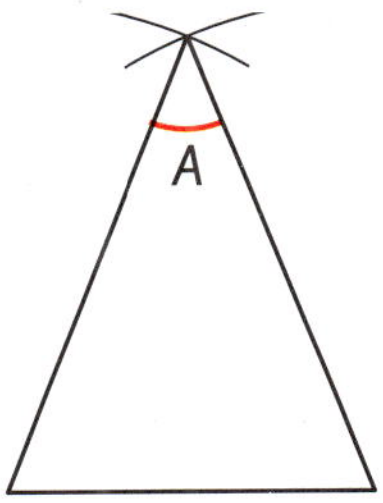

Join up the completed diagram.

B5 Measure the angle A at the top of the frame. Did you get 44°?

B6 Use the same method to construct these triangles. (**e** needs a different method) Write down the values of **a**, **b**, **c**, **d** and **e**.

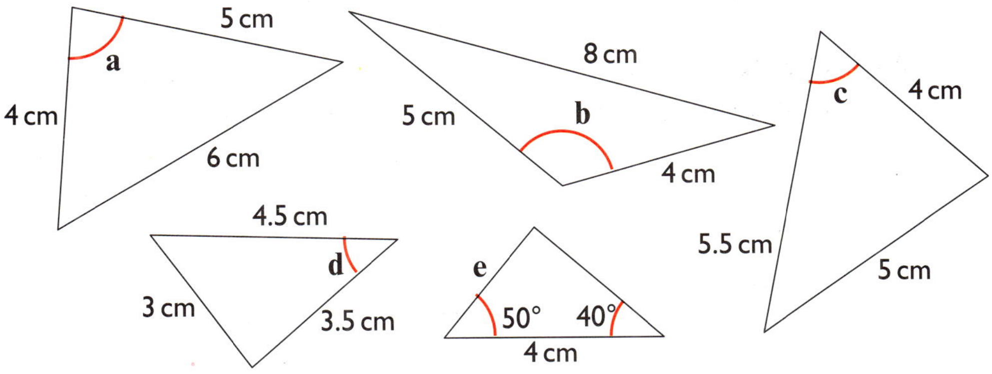

C Parallel lines

Parallel lines are straight lines that never meet. (Parallel lines can be curved like railway lines.)

Here is a pile of sticks:

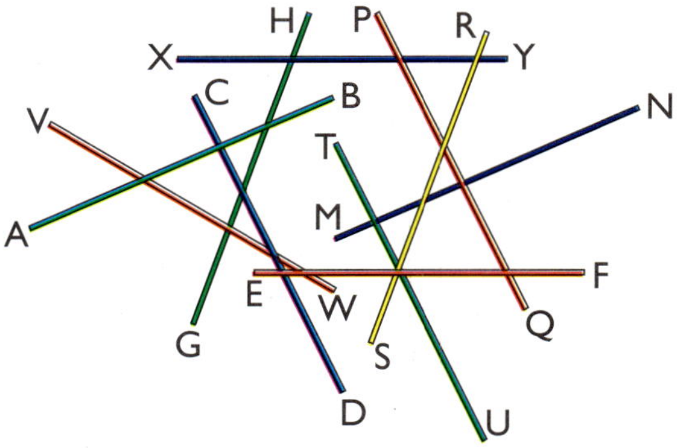

C1 Which stick is parallel to the stick AB?

C2 There are two sticks parallel to CD. Which are they?

C3 Which other pairs of sticks are parallel?

C4 Which stick is not parallel to any of the others?

To construct straight parallel lines accurately, you need a **set square**.

C5 Follow these instructions to draw straight parallel lines 3 cm apart:

a

Draw a line AB about 6 cm long, as shown.

b

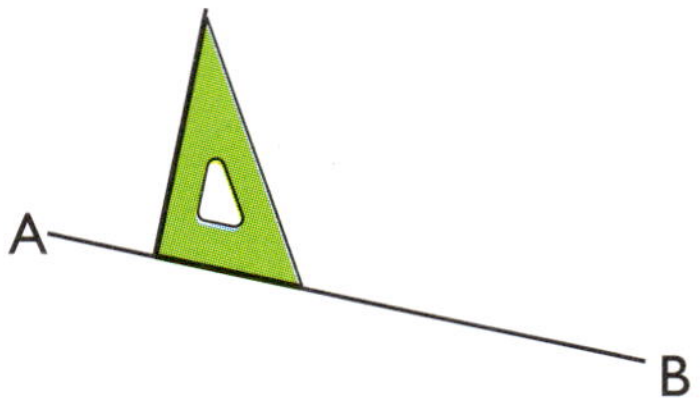

Put your set square on the line AB near A. Draw a line at right angles to AB.

c

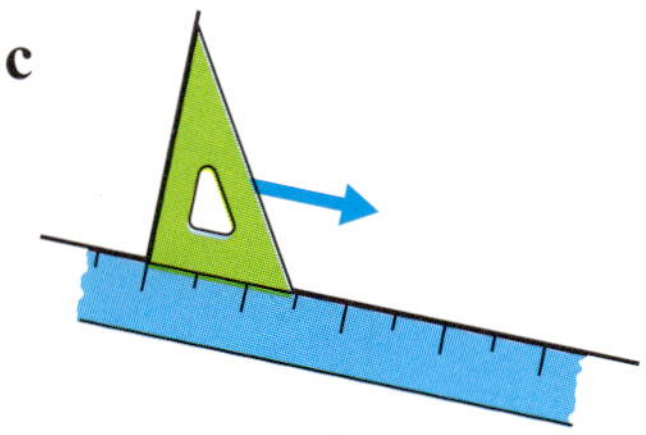

Replace your ruler along AB. Slide the set square along the ruler.

d

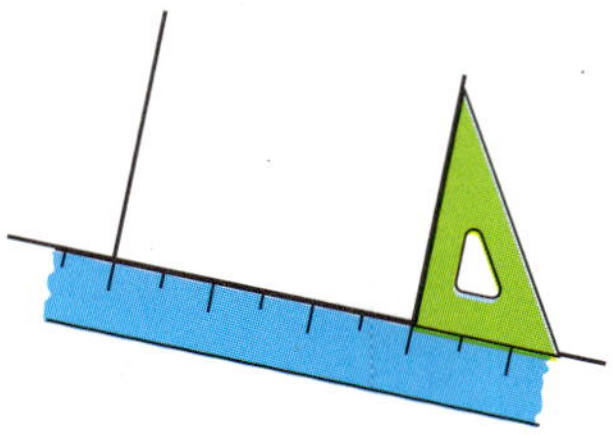

Move the set square 3 cm from its original position and draw a parallel line.

C6 A triangular rose bed is to be surrounded by a path 2 metres wide, as shown in the diagram.

Construct the triangle accurately using a scale of 1 cm to 1 m and draw parallel lines around the triangle to show the path.

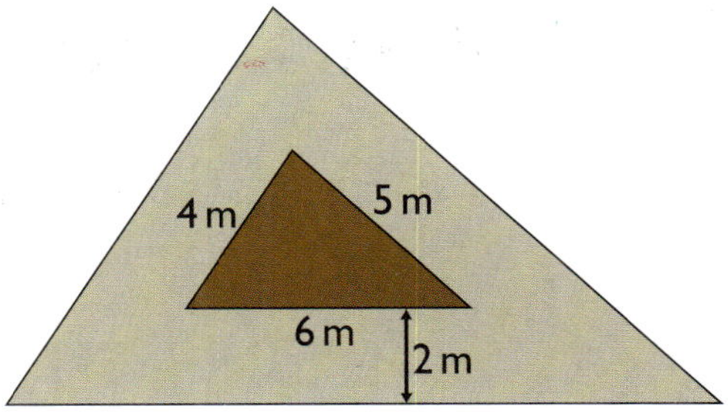

After the plans for the path around the rose bed were drawn, it was felt that the corners looked unattractive. It was agreed that they should be rounded so that the path was always 2 m wide.

Altering the plan was not difficult. The parallel lines round the triangle were drawn as before, but at each corner, compasses set at radius 2 cm were used to 'round' the corner.

The new drawing looks like this:

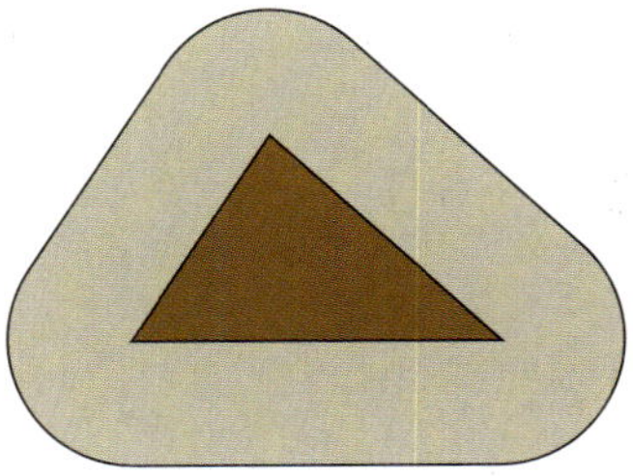

C7 Draw the triangular rose bed, using the same scale as before, with rounded corners.

You will notice that the edge of the path is always 2 metres from the rose bed. We call this the **locus** of points 2 metres from the rose bed.

A locus is a set of all points which follow a definite rule.

C8 Draw each of these flower beds accurately. By drawing parallel lines and arcs of circles, form the locus of points 2 m from the bed.
Use a scale of 1 cm to represent 1 m.
(You will need a pair of compasses, a ruler, a protractor and a set square.)

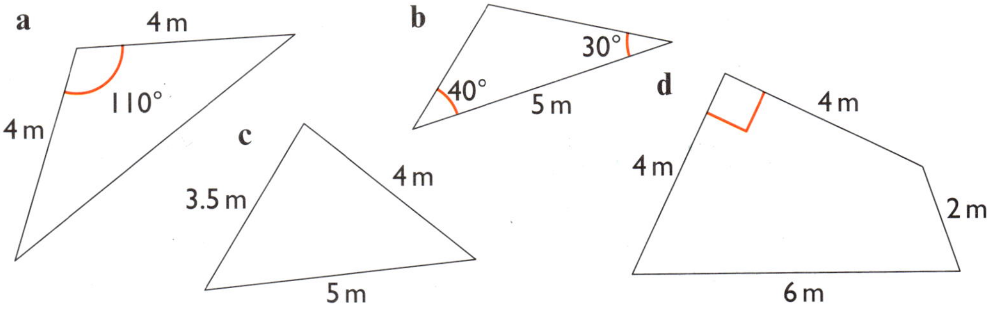

D Flying high

'We are pleased to announce the early arrival of the flight from New York. This is due to favourable weather conditions.'

Long distance flights sometimes arrive early because the winds are in a favourable direction.

D1 What would happen if the winds were in the opposite direction?

We can show the course followed by an aircraft on paper.

D2 A plane flies north-east at 500 miles per hour. The wind blows to the east at 100 mph. The sketch shows the distance d travelled by the plane in one hour.

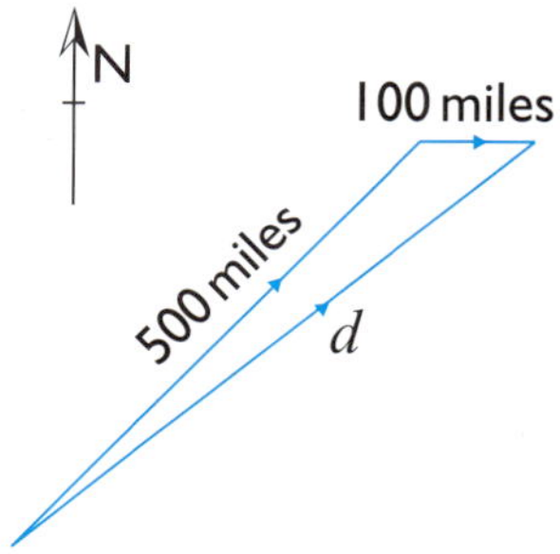

Make an accurate drawing to work out how far the plane has travelled in one hour.

D3 How far does the plane travel in two hours?

D4 Draw scale diagrams to solve each of these. First sketch the information and then draw it accurately using a scale of 1 cm to 100 miles.

a A plane flies north at 600 mph. The wind blows to the north-east at 150 mph. How far does the plane travel in one hour?

b A plane flies west at 550 mph. The wind blows to the south-west at 100 mph. How far does the plane travel in one hour?

c A plane flies south-west at 350 mph. The wind blows to the east at 150 mph. How far does the plane travel in one hour?

d A plane flies south-east at 600 mph. The wind blows to the north-east at 60 mph. How far does the plane travel in one hour?

D5 This sketch shows the route for a sailing competition.

Starting from the buoy at A, yachts must sail around the other buoys at B, C and D and finish at A.

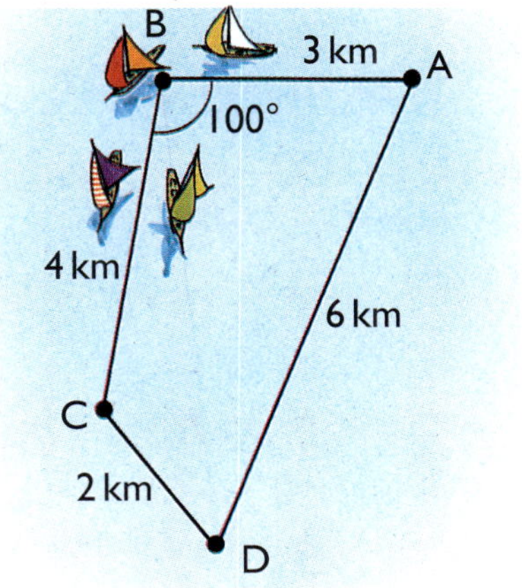

a Draw an accurate scale plan of the route to be taken. Use a scale of 1 cm to 1 km.

b Another yacht was disqualified because it travelled from B to D, missing out C. By measuring your scale drawing, how much shorter was this route?

c In a second race, the route travelled was from A to C to D, finishing at B. How far was this race?

D6 As he swam across a river 300 m wide, the current took Ashmed 200 m down the river.

This is shown in the diagram.

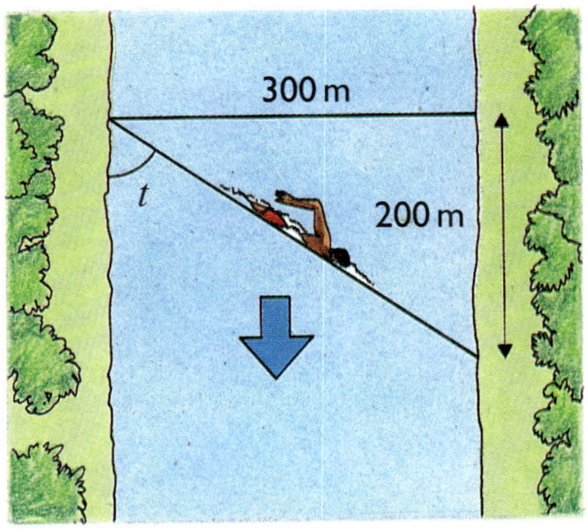

a Draw an accurate diagram using a scale of 1 cm to represent 50 m.

b From your scale drawing, work out:

i how far Ashmed swam

ii the angle that Ashmed swam to the river bank (marked *t*).

Two guides are completing their Silver Duke of Edinburgh Award, walking from Avasack to Billican, a distance of 24 km. After 4 hours, they realize that they are 14 km from Avasack, but still 16 km from Billican.

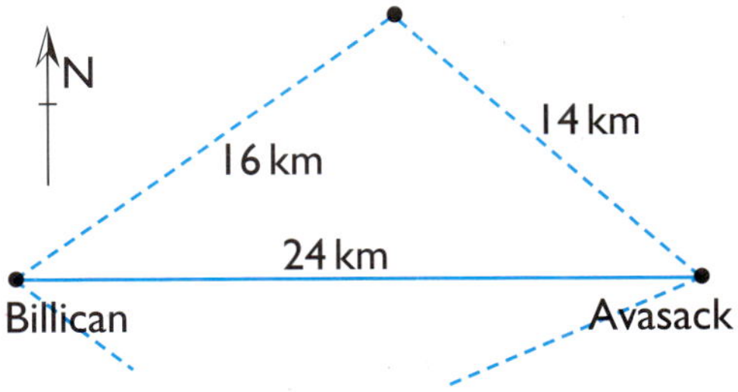

D7 By making a scale drawing, show that there are two possible positions where the guides can be. Use a scale of 1 cm to 2 km.

D8 They walk a further 14 km and find themselves due south of Billican. Show this position on your scale diagram.
What is the distance that they could be from Billican?

E Estimation through scale drawing

The Venture Scout group were at a weekend camp. On Saturday morning, they were set a number of tasks, each involving a scale drawing.

They had to estimate the height of a tower.

The first group used a protractor and a tape measure. They measured a distance of 50 m from the tower and then measured an angle of elevation of 20° from the horizontal to the top of the tower.

Here is their sketch:

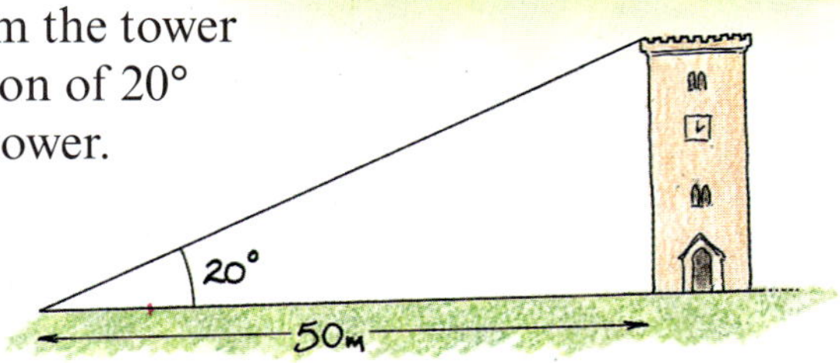

E1 Make a scale drawing using this information. Use a scale of 1 cm to 5 m. How high is the tower using these measurements?

A second group had not brought a protractor. They only had a tape measure. They estimated the height of the tower using a different method.

Esther knew she was 175 cm or 1.75 m tall. By lining the top of her head with the top of the tower, the group made this sketch:

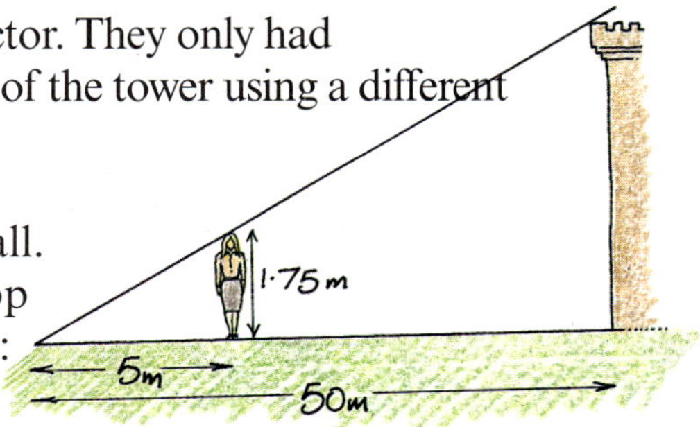

E2 Make a scale drawing using this information. Use a scale of 1 cm to 5 m which makes Esther's height 3.5 mm. How high is the tower using these measurements? (You will need to draw a small triangle with Esther first and then continue the lines.)

E3 Can you explain why the answers to questions **E1** and **E2** are different? What could have gone wrong?

Another task was to estimate the width of a river. The first group again used a protractor, but the second group did not. Here are their rough sketches:

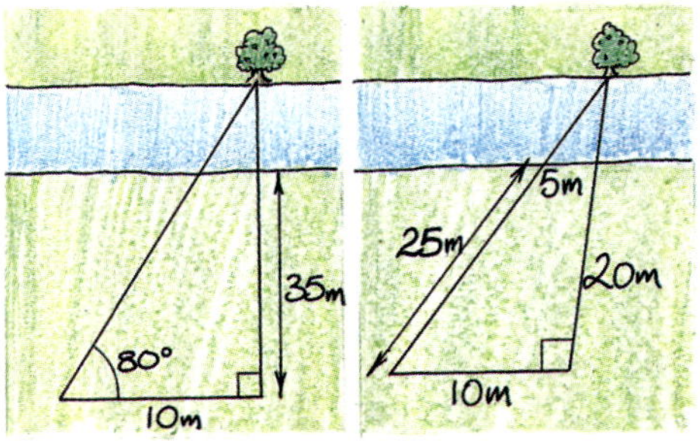

E4 Draw both of these accurately. Use a scale of 1 cm to 5 m. How wide do you think the river was?

F Polypatterns – Extension work

angle measurer or 360° protractor

You need an angle measurer or 360° protractor. Your task is to draw all the regular polygons from 3-sided to 10-sided. For each polygon, divide the angle at the centre (360°) by the number of sides.

For example, to draw a regular 6-sided polygon (hexagon), divide 360° by 6.
360° ÷ 6 = 60°.

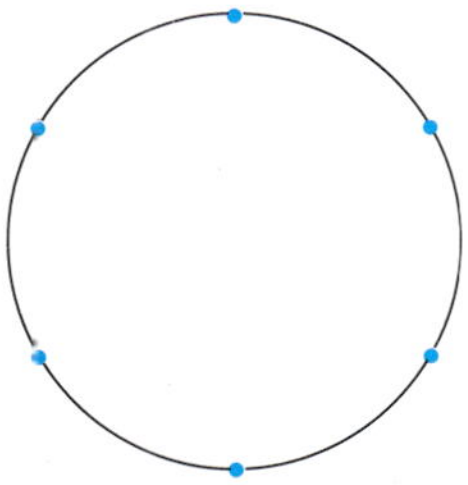

Place a 360° protractor on your paper. Mark dots every 60° for 0° as shown.

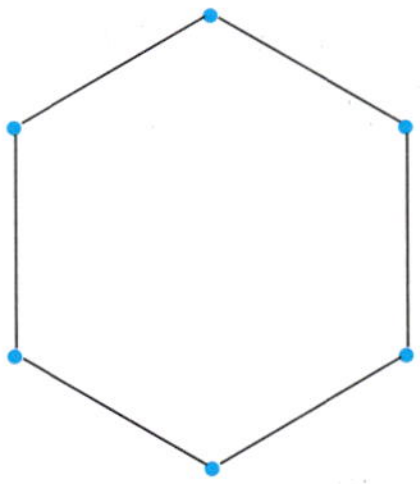

Join up the dots.

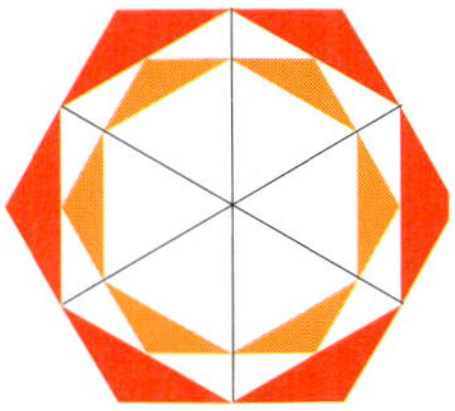

Put the protractor over a corner of the completed hexagon. Measure the inside angle (called the interior angle). It should be 120°.

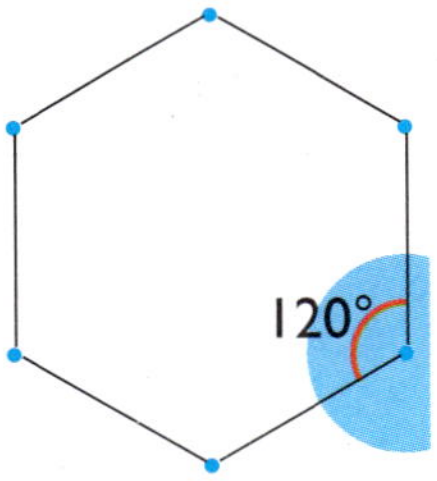

F1 Use the same method to draw all the regular polygons up to 10 sides.

F2 Copy and complete the table.

Number of sides	Name of polygon	Size of interior angle
3	triangle	60°
4		
5		
6	hexagon	120°
7		
8		
9	nonagon	
10		

F3 **a** Change your polygons into the polypatterns which decorate this page.

b Describe the order of rotational symmetry of your polypatterns.

UNIT 6 Commonsense measuring

A Length

In the metric system, the basic measurement is the metre which is made up of 100 centimetres.

To measure very small lengths, such as the width of your little finger nail, the centimetre is divided into 10 millimetres.
For longer lengths, 1000 metres make a kilometre.

10 millimetres (mm) = 1 centimetre (cm)
100 centimetres (cm) = 1 metre (m)
1000 metres (m) = 1 kilometre (km)

A1 Write down the most suitable unit for measuring:

a the length of the classroom

b the distance from London to Edinburgh

c the width of your pen.

A2 Estimate the following lengths, giving appropriate units:

a the length of a mini-bus

b the height of the classroom

c the thickness of your ruler.

Metric weights and measures started to be used widely in Britain after 1965. Before that, most measurements were made using imperial units, often based on body measurements.

The common imperial units of length are the inch, the foot, the yard and the mile.

The foot is based on the length of a human foot, the yard on the length of a stride and the mile (from Roman times) on 1000 strides.

The foot is divided into 12 inches.

12 inches = 1 foot
3 feet = 1 yard
1760 yards = 1 mile

The approximate metric equivalents of imperial units are:

1 inch ≈ 2.5 cm
1 foot ≈ 30 cm
1 yard ≈ 91 cm
1 km ≈ $\frac{5}{8}$ mile
5 miles ≈ 8 km

A3 Write down the approximate metric equivalent of:

a 4 inches **b** 100 miles

c 100 yards **d** 25 feet

A4 Write down the approximate imperial equivalent of:

a 80 cm **b** 1 metre

c 100 metres **d** 5 cm

A5 Which is longer?

a 1 mile or 1 kilometre

b 1 metre or 1 yard

c 1 centimetre or 1 inch

A6 What is a suitable metric speed limit to use instead of 30 miles per hour? Remember it should be rounded to the nearest 10 kilometres per hour.

B Area

B1 To find the area of your classroom, you would probably use square metres. Remind yourself what a square metre looks like by marking it out.

What units would you use to find the area of:

a the page of your book

b the fingernail of your little finger

c a leaf

d a playing field

e a table top

f the country in which you live?

For **large areas**, the metric system uses **hectares** where:

1 hectare = 10 000 square metres

but we still frequently use **acres** where:

1 acre = 4840 square yards

The acre dates back to the time of the Romans. Originally, it was the amount of land a pair of oxen could plough in a day.

B2 Find out which is bigger, a hectare or an acre.
Roughly how many acres are there in a hectare or how many hectares are there in an acre?
(You will need to know that 1 yard is about 0.91 m.)

B3 A field is rectangular and measures 120 m by 130 m.
Find its area in hectares. Roughly how many acres is this?

B4 A square piece of land has an area of 4 hectares.
What is the length of one side of this piece of land?

B5 A builder wishes to buy some land.
One site is available at £750 per acre.
A similar site is available at £1850 per hectare.
Which site is the better buy?

B6 Select one of your school games pitches (e.g. hockey, football, tennis) and *estimate* its area in hectares and in acres.
Then either measure, or find out, its actual area.

B7 How many 10 cm by 10 cm tiles would be needed to cover:

a the floor of the classroom

b the games pitch in question **B6**

c the top of the table or desk where you are working?

In each case, make an estimate first before you calculate.

C Volume and capacity

We normally measure **volume** in cubic millimetres, cubic centimetres or cubic metres (mm^3, cm^3, m^3) where:

$1\,m^3 = 1\,000\,000\,cm^3 = 1\,000\,000\,000\,mm^3$

but it is usual to measure fluids by using the **capacity** of a container in litres, centilitres or millilitres (ℓ, $c\ell$, $m\ell$):

$1\,\ell = 100\,c\ell = 1000\,m\ell$

Note: $1\,\ell = 1000\,cm^3$ and so $1\,m\ell = 1\,cm^3$ (sometimes abbreviated cc).

Often, you will find imperial units still in use (imperial means from the British Empire, although many units date back to the Roman Empire):

20 fluid ounces (fl oz) = 1 pint (pt)

8 pints = 1 gallon (gal)

C1 1 gallon is equivalent to 4.545 litres.

a Convert 1 pint to litres (correct to 3 decimal places).

b Write down a sensible rough approximation for a pint in $m\ell$.

C2 A motorist uses 1000 gallons of petrol.
Convert this to litres.

C3 Suggest suitable units to measure the capacity of:

a a teaspoon

b a bucket

c a cup

d a petrol storage tank in a garage

e a car's petrol tank.

C4 Suggest suitable units to measure the volume of:

a a suitcase

b your classroom

c a Post Office delivery van

d a bar of soap

e a football.

C5 Find three containers (e.g. bucket, jug, mug) and *estimate* their capacities in both pints and litres.

Now *measure* their capacities.

C6 Estimate the volume of your body.

How could it be measured?

C7 Work out the approximate volumes for:

a the inside of a car

b your classroom

c a room in your home.

C8 If you filled your classroom with water (assuming it did not leak!), how many litres would it hold?

How many pints would this be?

D Mass and weight

The **mass** of an object is 'the quantity of matter in the object'.

The **weight** of an object is the downward force on it due to gravity.

For a particular object, its mass is always the same, but its weight varies according to the force of gravity. On the Moon, where gravity is less than on Earth, its weight would therefore be smaller, but the amount of matter (the mass) would be the same.

The following units are, strictly speaking, for mass but, in everyday life, they are used for both mass and weight. A **kilogram** is the mass of a litre of water, but is commonly used as a unit of weight.

1 tonne (t) = 1000 kilograms (kg)
1 kilogram = 1000 grams (g)
1 gram = 1000 milligrams (mg)

We still use imperial units for weight, particularly the pound (lb) and the ounce (oz) where:

16 ounces = 1 pound

Note: 1 lb is about 0.454 kg or 454 g.

D1 How many pounds are there in a kilogram? What is a sensible rough approximation?

D2 Two shops get potatoes from the same supplier. In one shop they are sold at 11p per pound and in the other at 27p per kilogram.

Which shop gives the better value?

D3 Which is numerically bigger, your height in centimetres or your weight in pounds?

Make an estimate and then find out.

D4 Suggest suitable units for the weight of:

a a paper clip

b a car

c a book

d an aeroplane

e a cat.

D5 A manufacturer's lorries are not licensed to carry more than 15 tonnes each. (Remember: 1 tonne = 1000 kg and 1 lb = 0.454 kg)

He wants to transport:

2000 boxes each weighing 11 kg
1000 boxes each weighing 54 lb
3000 boxes each weighing 15 kg
4000 boxes each weighing 60 lb.

a How many lorries will he need?

b Work out a plan showing exactly what each lorry should carry. There may be more than one possible plan. Give reasons for your method of loading.

D6 Find the weights and prices of three different boxes of chocolates.

Calculate the best buy in terms of pence per gram.

E Accuracy and errors

E1 Look at these statements. Some of them are not sensible.

a The train takes 2 hours 24 minutes 35 seconds to get to London.

b I live 1 976 876.7 cm from school.

c The sun is 93 000 000 miles from the Earth.

d The room is 4251.63 mm long.

e My car's petrol tank holds 50 litres to the nearest 10 litres.

f The piece of paper is 0.135 mm thick.

Which of the statements seem sensible?
Rewrite the others so that they are also sensible.

E2 Suggest the degree of accuracy which is appropriate for the following measurements (e.g. 'nearest cm', 'nearest litre' etc.):

a the number of people at a football match

b your height

c the height of the tallest building in London

d the weight of a bus

e the area of the walls in your classroom

f the time taken to boil an egg

g the time taken to fly from London to Tokyo

h the cost of a house.

Extension work

E3 A carpet fitter always measures to the nearest centimetre above the actual length being measured. (This is called **rounding up**.)

If a carpet is being fitted in a rectangular room and the fitter's order is based on measurements of 505 cm and 324 cm, what is the maximum area of the carpet that could be wasted?

What percentage of the total carpet is this wasted area?

E4 A factory produces nails at a rate of 2500 per hour to the nearest 50.

In a 38-hour working week, what is:

a the greatest number of nails that would be produced

b the least number

c the difference between the greatest and the least over a period of a 50-week year?

E5 Jeremy orders tiles to cover an area of 10 m^2 in his bathroom.

The tiles each measure 4 cm by 4 cm, but Jeremy mistakenly assumed that they were 4 inches by 4 inches.
(1 inch is approximately 2.54 cm.)

a How many tiles with the correct measurements should Jeremy have ordered?

b How many tiles did he order instead?

c By how many was he short or did he have too many?

UNIT 7 Polygons

A Polygons around us

Polygons are flat or plane shapes with three or more straight sides and, of course, the same number of angles. They form a closed loop.

The name polygon comes from the Greek words 'polys' meaning 'many' and 'gonia' meaning 'angle'. The sides need not be of equal lengths.

You have met the more familiar polygons before. They are:

triangle
(meaning 3 angles)

quadrilateral
(meaning 4 sides)

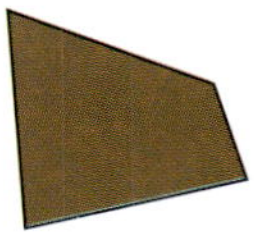

pentagon
(meaning 5 angles)

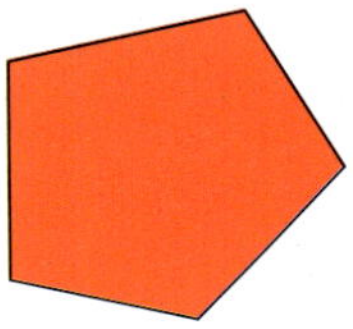

hexagon
(meaning 6 angles)

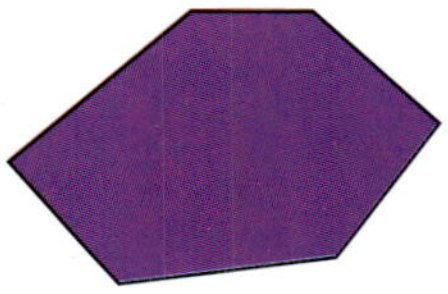

octagon
(meaning 8 angles)

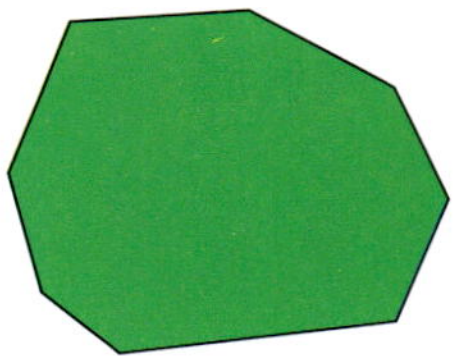

dodecagon
(meaning 12 angles)

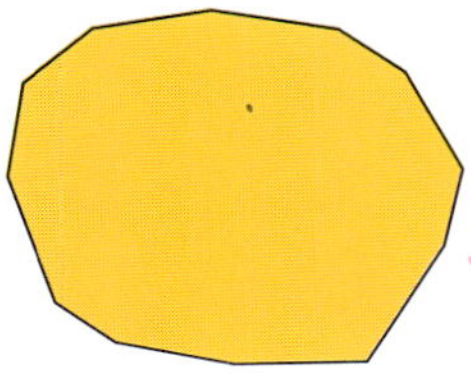

A1 Find out the names of the polygons which have 7, 9 and 10 sides (if you did not answer question **F2** on page 50). Draw sketches of them.

A2 Name the polygons which appear in the photographs below:

a

This famous building belongs to the Department of Defense in the USA.

b

A bee's honeycomb.

A3 This is a picture of part of the ceiling of the Central Lobby in the Houses of Parliament.

List as many different polygons as you can find in the picture.

A4 Now look for some different polygons of your own.
Look for pictures in magazines and newspapers.
Look around your school buildings – at walls, gates and paving stones for example.
Make a list of the polygons you have found and where you found them.

Convex and concave polygons

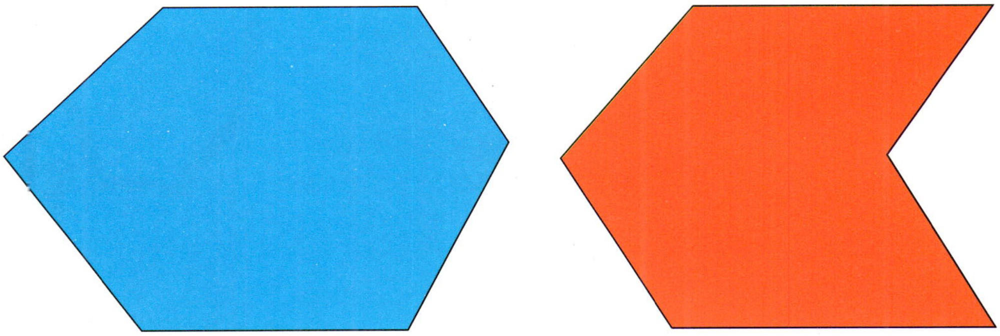

Both these shapes are hexagons.
The one on the left is **convex**, the one on the right is **concave**.

A5 Describe the differences between them.

A6 This shape is similar to the Star of David, the symbol used in the Jewish faith.
It is also a dodecagon.

Is the star convex or concave?

B The construction of convex polygons

geostrips
paper fasteners

You will need 'geostrips' of various lengths. These may be commercially produced or home-made from strips of plastic or card with holes near the ends. You will also need some paper-fasteners.

Join three geostrips together to form a triangle using paper-fasteners.

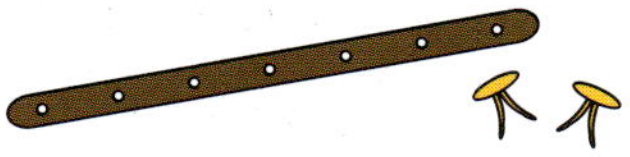

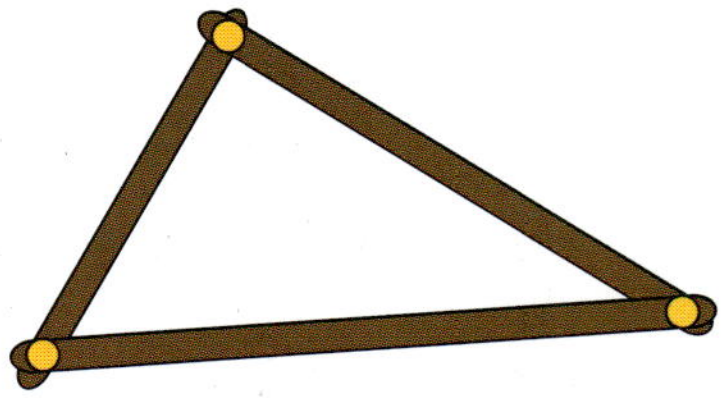

B1 What do the angles of a triangle add up to? Is the shape rigid?

Join four geostrips together to form a quadrilateral.

You should notice that the shape will move to form many different quadrilaterals.

To make a rigid shape, add an extra geostrip to make a diagonal.

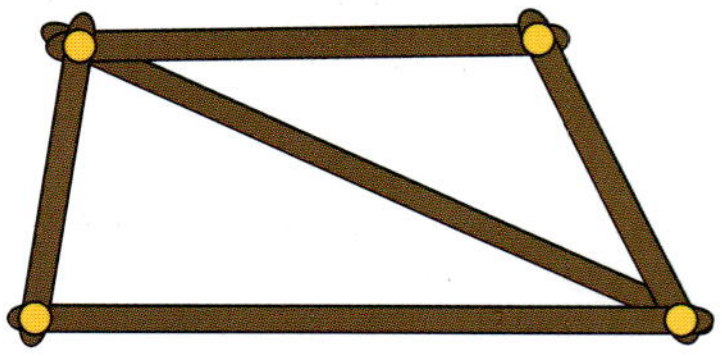

B2 Using the fact that each triangle contains 180°, what do the angles of a quadrilateral add up to?

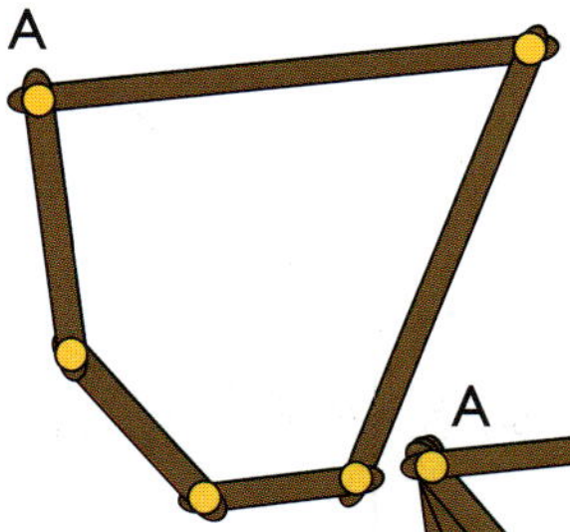

Join five strips together to make a pentagon.

To make your pentagon rigid, add two diagonals from A to the other corners as shown.

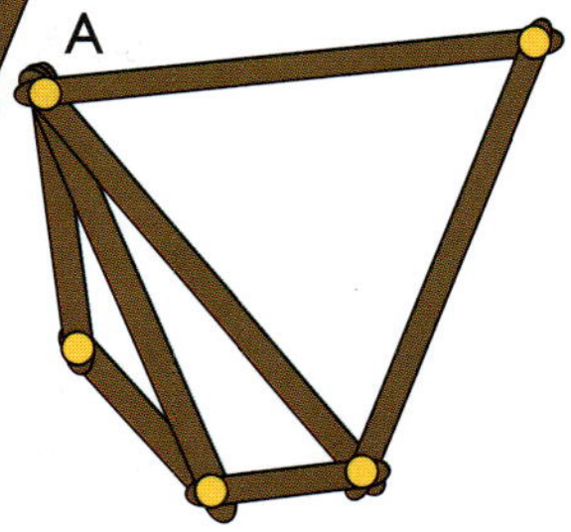

B3 **a** How many triangles are there in your rigid pentagon?

b What do the angles of a pentagon add up to?

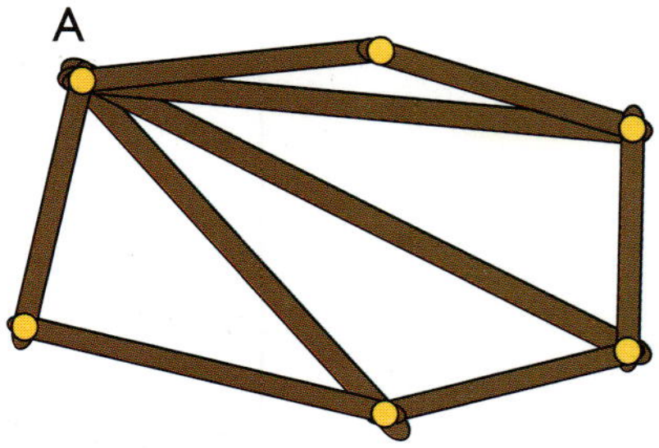

B4 Construct a hexagon (6 sides), heptagon (7 sides) and octagon (8 sides) in the same way. Make each shape rigid by adding diagonals as before but be sure that they all come from one corner A of the polygon.

B5 Copy and complete this table:

Name of polygon	Number of sides	Number of diagonals	Number of triangles	Sum of angles
triangle	3	0	1	1 × 180 = 180
quadrilateral	4	1	2	2 × 180 = 360
pentagon	5	2	3	3 × 180 =
decagon	10			

B6 Find a rule between the number of sides and the number of triangles.

B7 Find a rule between the number of sides and the sum of all the angles inside the polygon.

B8 What is the sum of the angles for a 20-sided polygon?

B9 Use the results from your table to calculate the angles marked with letters. (Note: these diagrams have not been drawn accurately.)

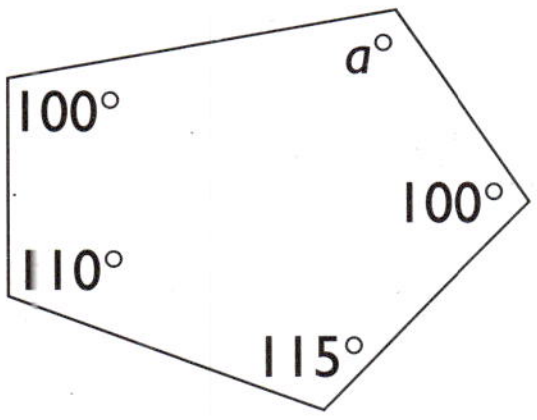

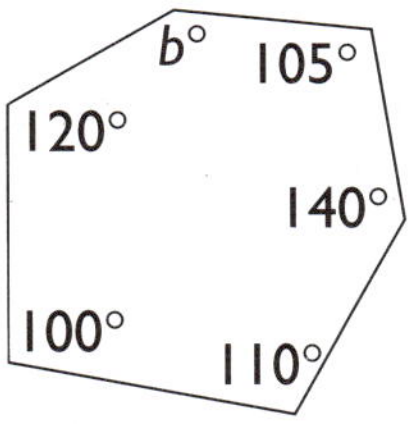

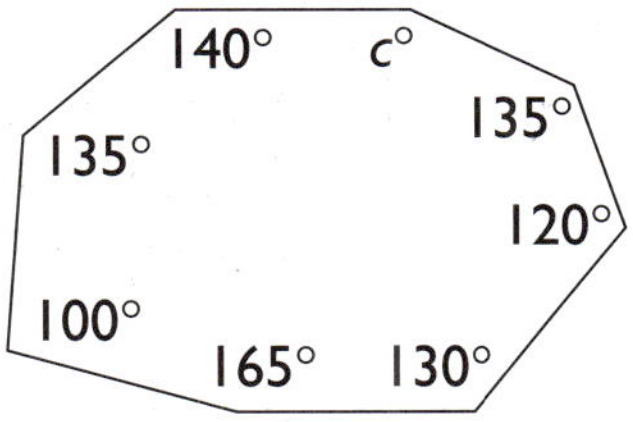

C Exterior angles

The exterior angles of the polygon below have been shaded.

The sides of the polygon have been extended in the same sense; they have all been extended in a clockwise sense.

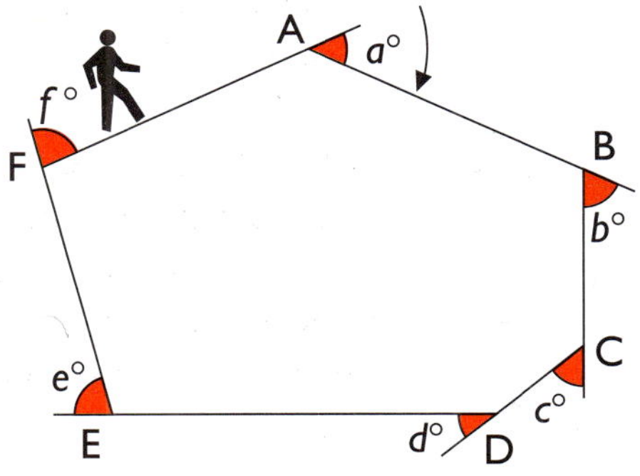

Imagine a garden path in the shape of a polygon.

You are walking round the path starting at F and walking towards A.

At A you will turn through an angle of a° and then walk towards B.

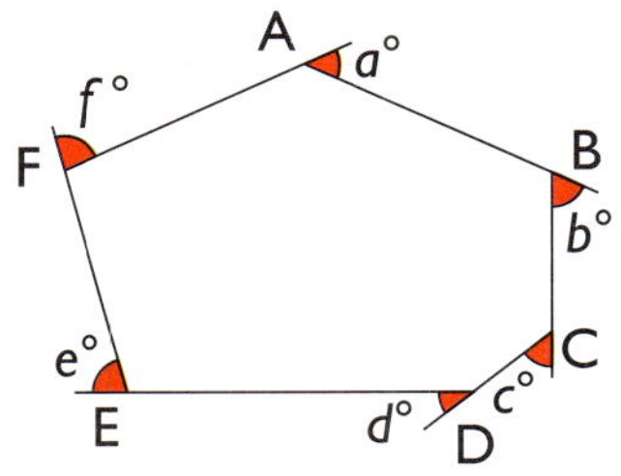

At B you will need to turn through $b°$ and walk towards C, and so on until you get back to your starting point.

As you are pointing in the direction in which you started, you have made a complete turn. You have turned through 360°.

So $a° + b° + c° + d° + e° + f° = 360°$.

You can see that:

The sum of the exterior angles of *any* polygon is 360°.

C1 Calculate the angles marked by letters in the diagrams below. (Note: the diagrams have not been drawn accurately.)

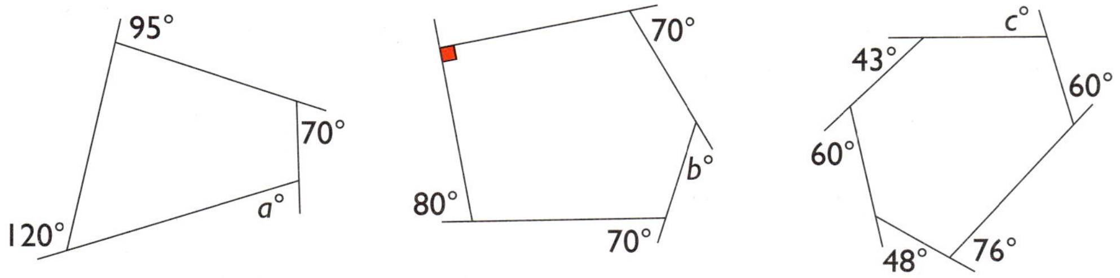

D Regular polygons

A regular polygon has all its sides *and* all its angles equal.

An equilateral triangle is a regular triangle – it has three equal sides and all its angles are 60°.

A square is a regular quadrilateral – it has four equal sides and all its angles are 90°.

D1 Which of the polygons below **i** are regular
ii have rotational symmetry?
(Give the order of rotational symmetry.)

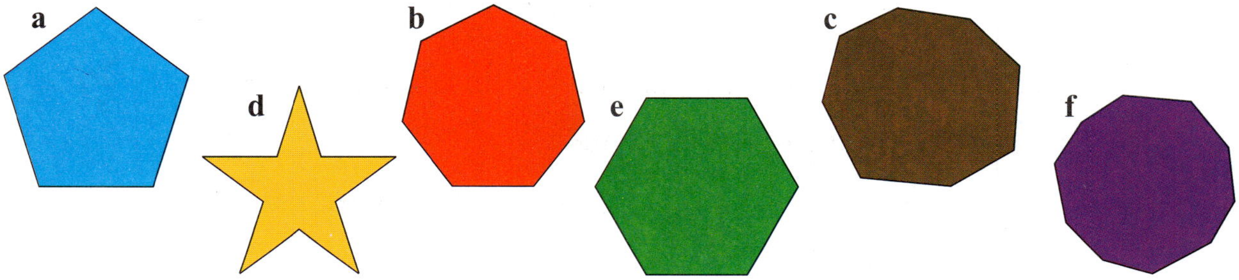

The construction of regular polygons

PQRST is a regular pentagon.

Note how the circle is used to draw it.

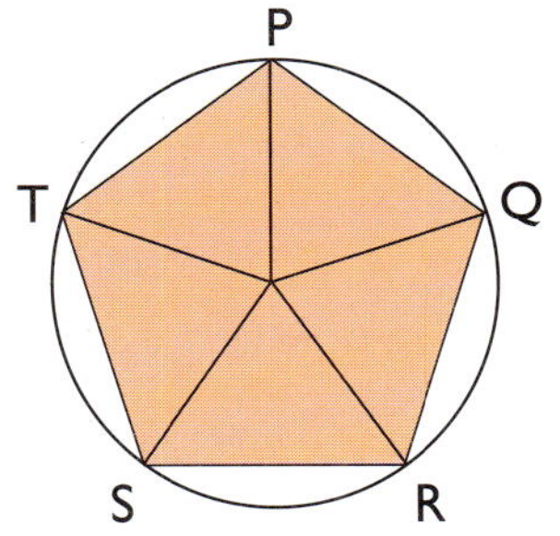

D2 What is the size of each of the five angles at the centre?

ABCDEF is a regular hexagon.

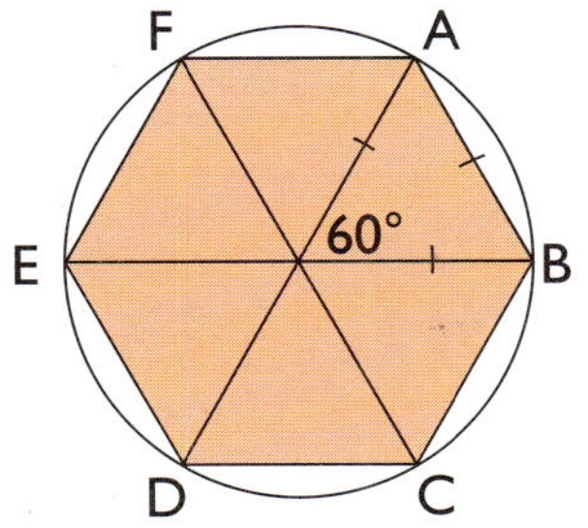

D3 Draw a regular hexagon, starting with a circle of radius 4 cm. This time you will have six angles at the centre, so each one will be 60°.

You will see that the triangles formed inside the regular hexagon are all equilateral. So the sides AB, BC and so on are all equal to the radius of the circle.

Measure yours to check!

This leads to a fast way of constructing a regular hexagon which you met earlier on page 26.

D4 Draw a circle of radius 5 cm.
Keep the compass at radius 5 cm.
Put the point on the circumference and draw an arc to cut the circumference at another point.
With the centre at this new point, draw another arc.
Repeat until six points are marked on the circle.
Join up the points to make a hexagon whose sides are the same length as the radius you started with.

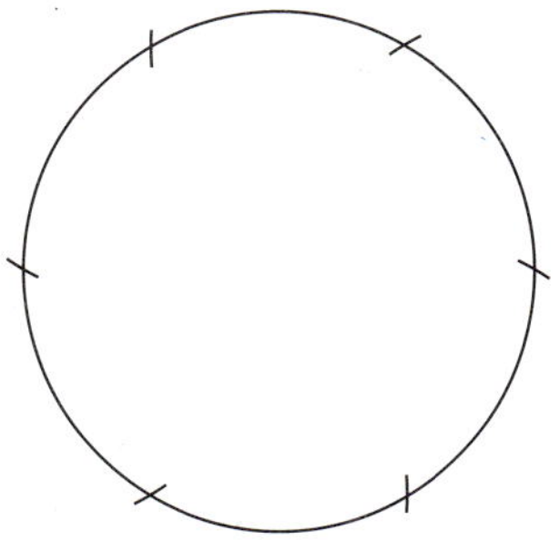

Other regular polygons can be drawn by using a circle and dividing the angle at the centre into the required number of parts.

D5 Draw a regular octagon and a regular decagon.

D6 The exterior angles of this regular octagon are shown.

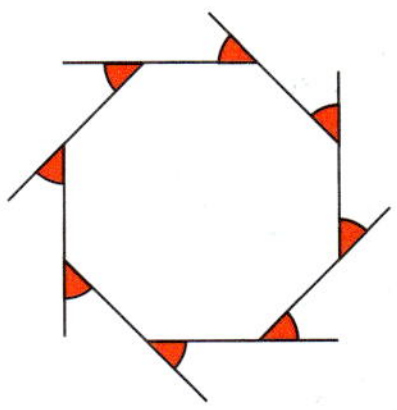

a How many exterior angles are there?

b As all the exterior angles add up to 360°, how large is one exterior angle?

D7 Repeat question **D6** using a regular decagon.

D8 Repeat question **D6** using a regular pentagon.

D9 This diagram shows the interior angle of a regular polygon.

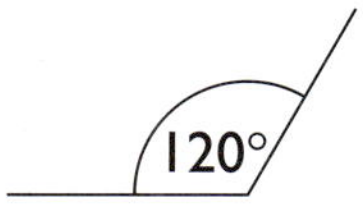

a How many sides does the regular polygon have?

b What do the interior and exterior angles add up to?

D10 How many sides has a regular polygon whose interior angle is 162°?

D11 Sketch an octagon which has equal sides but whose angles are not equal.

E More properties of regular polygons

Symmetry

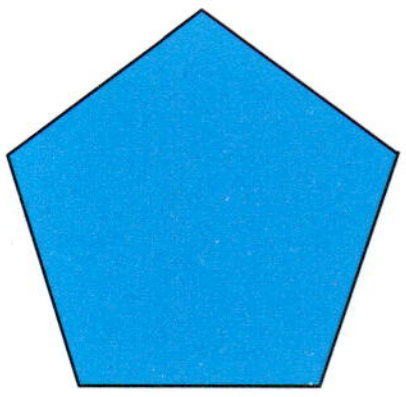

E1 **a** Copy this regular pentagon on to tracing paper.
Fold it along its lines of symmetry.
How many lines of symmetry does it have?

b Now place your copy over the one on the page. Hold it at the point where the folded lines cross (its centre) with a pencil point. Rotate it carefully about the centre to find the **order of rotational symmetry**; that is, how many times it fits exactly over the original pentagon.

c Draw the pentagon in your book and mark the lines of symmetry and the point of rotational symmetry.

E2 Repeat question **E1** for other regular polygons. Use some of the constructions you have made earlier to trace around. Work out mentally the number of lines of symmetry for a regular 20-gon.

Tessellations

Look back at the honeycomb at the beginning of this unit.
From this you will see that regular hexagons **tessellate**. That is to say, they fit together exactly, leaving no spaces.
Look at a piece of isometric grid paper. You will see from this that equilateral triangles also tessellate.

E3 **Investigation** Find out which other regular polygons tessellate.
Make at least six copies of the shape you wish to investigate.
For example, you may wish to explore pentagons by making six copies of the pentagon above and fitting them together.

You may find that a polygon will not tessellate on its own. Sometimes two polygons together make a shape which tessellates. Here is one made up of regular octagons and squares.

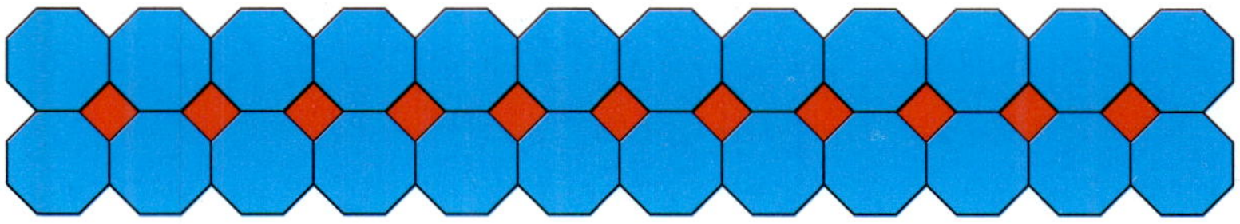

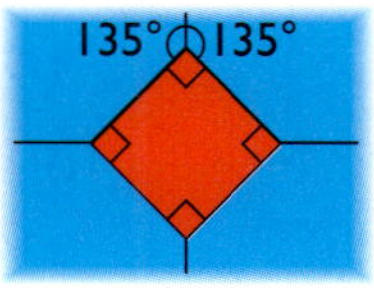

E4 By looking at the interior angles of these two regular polygons, explain why they tessellate. (Remember: it is important that there are no gaps.)

E5 Use a similar argument to explain why regular hexagons tessellate.

E6 By looking at the interior angles of other regular polygons, find more combinations which will tessellate.
Draw sketches to show your results.

F Another look at pentagons

F1 You can make a regular pentagon in a different way by knotting a strip of paper.

Take a strip of paper about 3 cm wide and 30 cm long. Carefully knot the paper as shown:

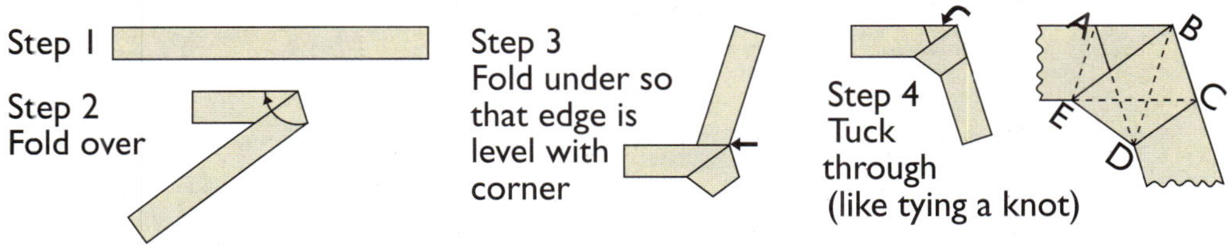

The points ABCDE form the vertices of a regular pentagon.

Now draw a line along AC and hold the knotted paper up to the light. You will see a star shape inside the pentagon.

The star is called a **pentagram**.

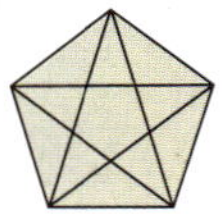

The ancient Greek mathematician called **Pythagoras** was born about 560 BC. He led an ancient secret sect called the Brotherhood. The members of this Brotherhood studied mathematics, magic and religion. They believed that 'All is number' and spent much of their time working out relationships between numbers in the world around them. They used the pentagram as their symbol. The pentagram is full of mathematical interest and is also used in some mystery books as a sign of wizards and magic.

G Pentominoes – Extension work

You will probably be familiar with the game of dominoes. Each **domino** is made from two squares joined by one complete side.

Now look at three squares. We can make a **tromino**. There are only two differently shaped trominoes.

Four squares make a **tetromino**. There are five of them.

(Note: if two shapes can be turned round or turned over to look identical, they count as the same shape.)

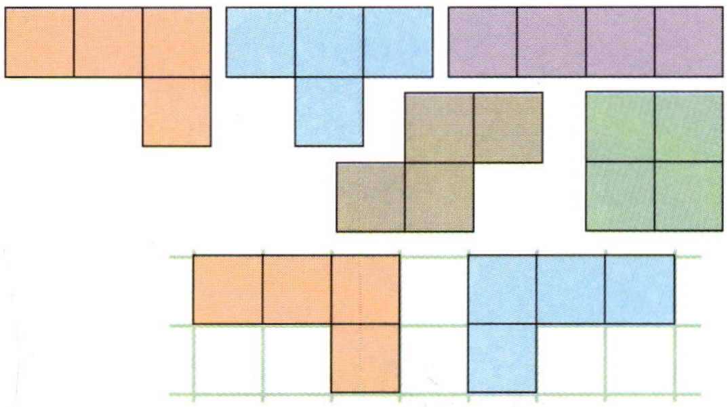

Five squares make a **pentomino**. Here are two pentominoes.

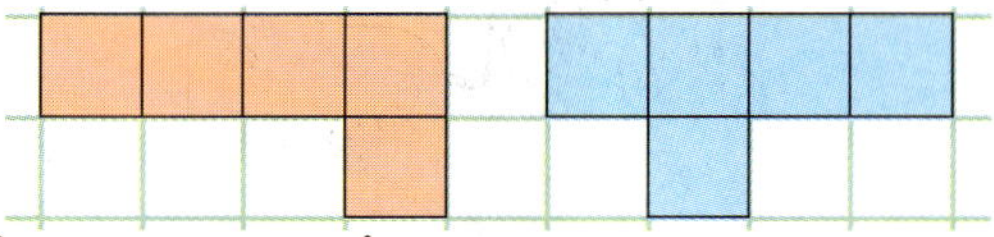

G1 Use squared paper to draw all 12 different pentominoes.

H Paper folding – Extension work

H1 Fold a piece of paper in two.
The fold forms a straight line or an angle of 180°.
Fold the paper again to get an angle of 90°.
Fold once more to get an angle of 45°.

Repeat this with four more pieces of paper so that you have five pieces of folded paper. Label them A to E.

Draw lines as indicated by the dotted red lines.

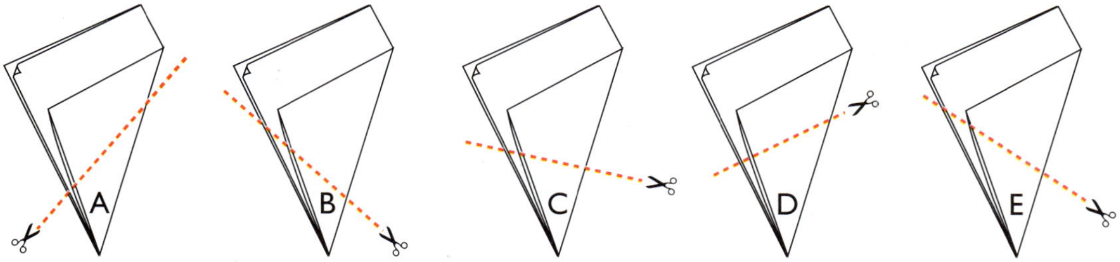

Before you cut along the dotted lines and open them, think about what shape you will get.

Decide, for each shape, if the opened shape will be regular and whether it will be convex or concave.

Cut and open. Were you right? Give each shape a name.

H2 Try folding the paper in different ways to get a six-pointed star.

Paper folding using circles

H3 Draw a circle of radius 5 cm and cut it out.

Fold in one part of the edge so that a point on the circumference just touches the centre.

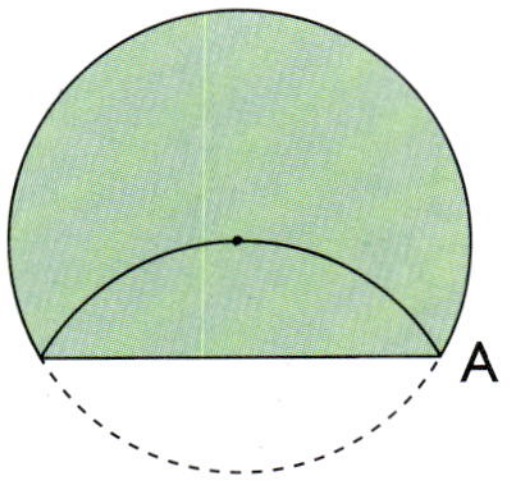

Then fold in another part of the edge starting at point A so that it just touches the centre.

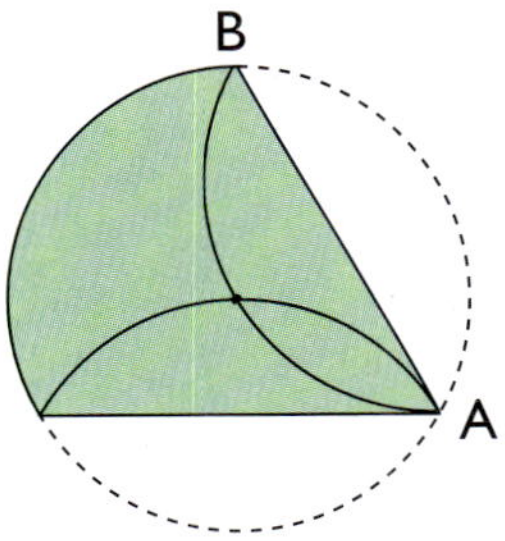

Repeat for the remaining part of the edge.

What shape do you get?

Hold it up to the light to see what pattern you get.

H4 Draw and cut out a circle of radius 9 cm.

Fold in one part of the edge so that a point on the circumference just touches the centre.

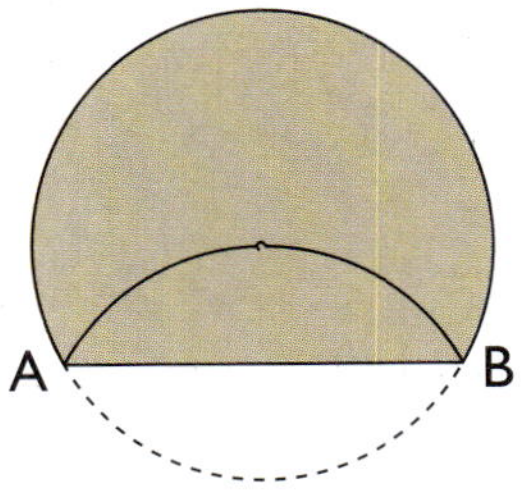

Now fold the point B to the centre.

Repeat with point C and continue until point A is folded in.

What shape do you get?

Use these folded shapes as templates to make tessellated patterns.

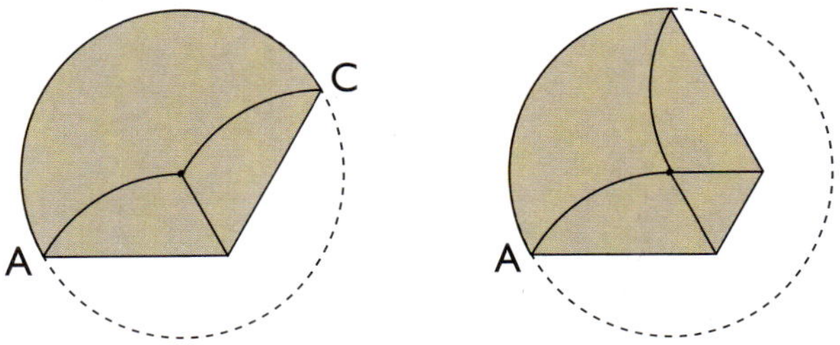

UNIT 8 Practical measuring

A Units of length

measuring tape

You need measuring rules and tapes which will measure metric and imperial units.

A1 Do this activity with a neighbour or in a small group.

a Draw a straight line.

Mark two points on the line.

Measure the distance between the two points as accurately as possible and record the length.

b Compare the length you have measured with those measured by other people in your group.

Did you all use the same units?

Use another unit of measure to record the length of your line.

Find at least three different units of measure to record the length of your line.

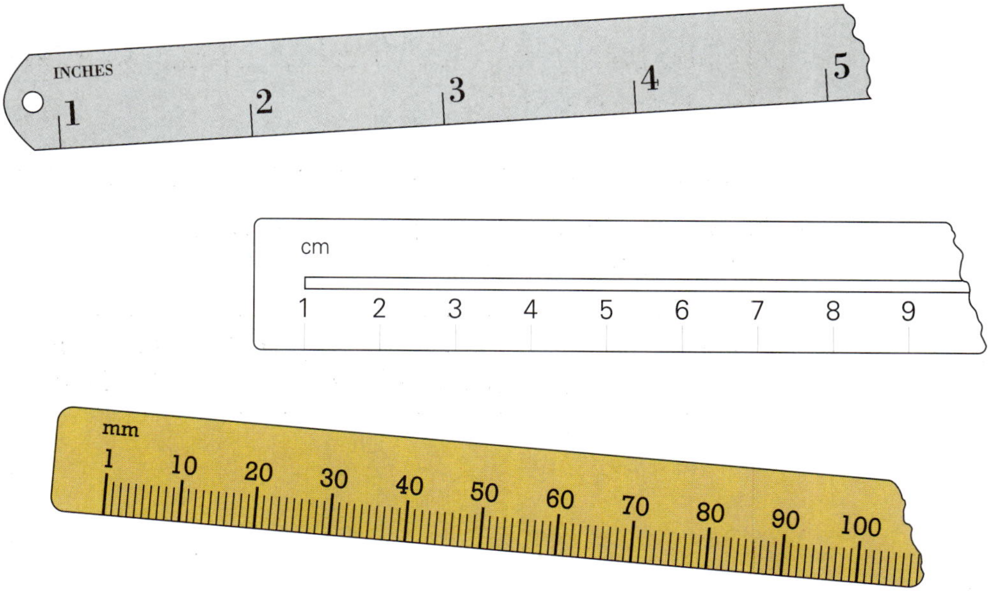

A2

a Measure this line in centimetres as accurately as you can and record the result.

b Now measure the length of the line in:

i millimetres

ii metres

iii inches

Are any of these units difficult to use?

c Which unit do you think is the best to use? Why?

stop watch
measuring tape

A3 Work in a group. Each group will need:

a stop watch

access to the school field or a sports track

measuring tapes.

You should aim to cover each distance at a steady pace. You are not racing against each other!

a Find the time it takes each member of your group to cover 100 m.

b Now copy this table or use Worksheet S2:5.
Fill in the first three columns.

S2:5

Name	Time to cover 100 m	Expected time for 1 km	Actual time for 1 km	Difference

How far is a kilometre?

The aim is for each member of your group to cover a kilometre in the expected time. The winner is the person who is closest to their expected time.

A4 Each group member should cover exactly one kilometre (decide carefully how you will measure this distance) and the times should then be recorded on the table in question **A3**.

Write down your thoughts about the 'kilometre journey' and comment on whether the actual times were generally greater or smaller than the expected times. If there is a difference, why do you think this is so?

How far is a mile?

S2:5

A5 **a** Copy this table or use Worksheet S2:5.

Name	Time taken to cover 100 m	Time taken to cover 100 yds	Time taken to cover 1 km	Expected time to cover 1 mile

Fill in columns 1, 2 and 4 from information you have already collected.

Work out (and fill in) columns 3 and 5.
(Note: 36 inches = 1 yard and 1760 yards = 1 mile)

b Do you think that the statement '1 kilometre is approximately $\frac{5}{8}$ mile' is a good one?

c Make a statement as accurately as you can about the relationship between kilometres and miles.

B Conversion graphs

B1 Design and make your own conversion graph for changing inches to centimetres. It should look something like this:

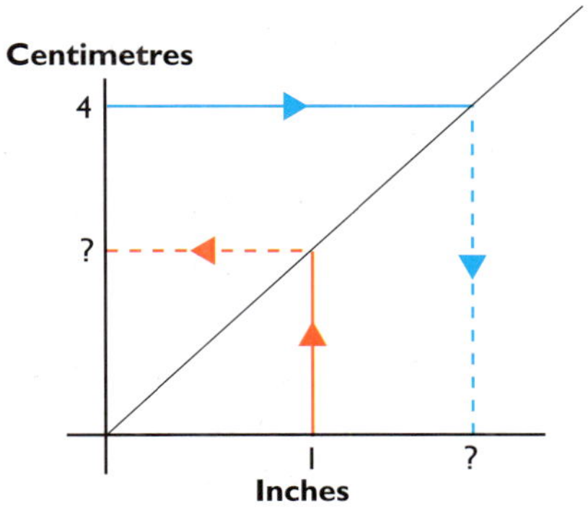

B2 Use your conversion graph to find, as accurately as possible, how many centimetres there are in the following lengths:

a 9 in **b** 15 in **c** 1 ft **d** 100 in

e 1 yd **f** 0.5 in **g** 0.25 in

B3 Use your conversion graph to find, as accurately as possible, how many inches there are in:

a 20 cm **b** 25 cm **c** 31 cm

d 1 m **e** 1.3 m **f** 1 cm

B4 Check your answers in questions **B2** and **B3** using appropriate rulers or measuring tapes.

B5 Design and make your own conversion graph for changing miles into kilometres.

B6 This chart shows distances in *miles* between some towns in the United Kingdom?

	London	Blackpool	Bournemouth	Cardiff	Dover	Edinburgh
Blackpool	226					
Bournemouth	100	270				
Cardiff	157	209	117			
Dover	71	297	174	238		
Edinburgh	378	183	439	385	449	
Oxford	57	187	90	105	129	357

For example, it is 297 miles from Blackpool to Dover.

Find the distances between:

a Bournemouth and Oxford **b** London and Edinburgh

c Cardiff and Edinburgh **d** Cardiff and Blackpool

e Which two places are furthest apart?

B7 **a** A family drives from Blackpool to Bournemouth and then to Dover. What is the length of their journey?

b How much shorter is it to go directly from Edinburgh to London rather than going from Edinburgh to London via Blackpool?

B8 Decide on a conversion rate from miles to kilometres and then rewrite the table of distances in kilometres, giving each distance to the nearest kilometre.

B9 You want to start from Oxford and visit Bournemouth, Dover and London before returning to Oxford. What is the shortest route you can take? Give details of the route and give the total distance in both miles and kilometres.

B10 The Olympic Marathon is 26 miles 385 yards long. What is this distance in kilometres to the nearest kilometre? What is the distance to the nearest metre?

C Units of weight

scales
metre rule
metre length of paper

You will need scales which weigh in metric units and imperial units and a metre ruler.

C1 The diagram shows you how the kilogram line from 0 to 1 can be filled in to give more detail.

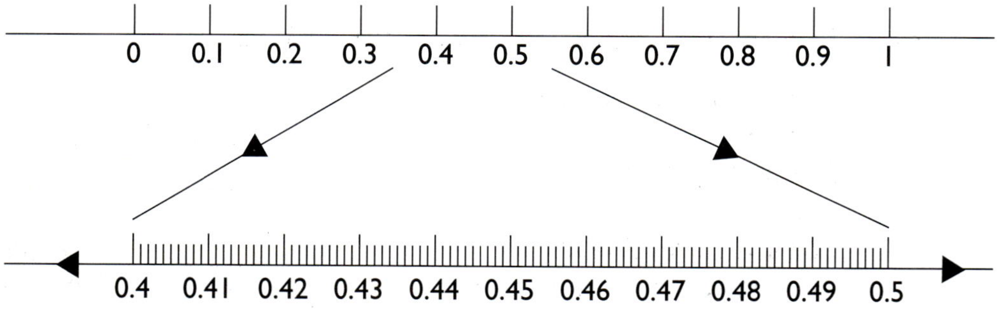

Make your own kilogram line. It should be one metre in length with the total length representing one kilogram. Label the hundredths of a kilogram.

Kilo is Greek for 1000. A kilogram is 1000 grams.

a What length on the line indicates a gram?

b Mark the grams between 0.4 and 0.5 kilograms and between 0 and 0.10 kilograms.

C2 Using any weights or weighing machines you have available, try to answer the following:

a How many grams are approximately equal to 1 ounce (oz)?

b How many grams are approximately equal to 1 pound (lb)?

c Check that your answer to **b** is approximately 16 times as big as your answer to **a**. Why should this be so?

d Put ounces and pounds on your kilogram number line.

C3 Copy and complete this table of approximate equivalent values:

Imperial unit	Metric unit
1 lb	
1 oz	
0.5 lb	
0.25 lb	
5 oz	
1.5 lb	
1.1 lb	
1.8 lb	
	0.5 kg
	1 kg
	400 g
	0.15 kg
	0.35 kg

C4 Here is a list of ingredients for nutty cookies:

4 oz full fat soft cheese
4 oz butter
3 oz caster sugar
1 egg
6 oz self-raising flour
2 oz toasted ground hazelnuts
2 oz raisins

a What is the total weight of the dry ingredients needed?

b If this recipe makes 24 biscuits, what would be the weight of dry ingredients needed to make:

i 72 biscuits **ii** 60 biscuits

c Convert all the quantities in the recipe to metric units (grams).

d What is the total weight of the dry ingredients in metric units?

D Liquid measure or capacity

D1 Make a list of ten liquids together with the volume by which they are usually sold.

For example: 1 pint of milk
1 litre of orange juice

1 litre = 1000 ml and 1 pint = 568 ml (approximately)

D2 Make your own chart, number line or ready reckoner which will enable you to convert from pints to litres or litres to pints. Use it to convert each of the volumes you listed in question **D1** to another unit of liquid measure.

D3 What volume does a **centilitre** represent? How many centilitres are there in:

a 1 litre

b 1 pint?

D4 A water tank has dimensions as shown.

a What is the volume in litres of the tank?

b If the tank was filled with water to a depth of 55 cm, how many litres of water would be in the tank?

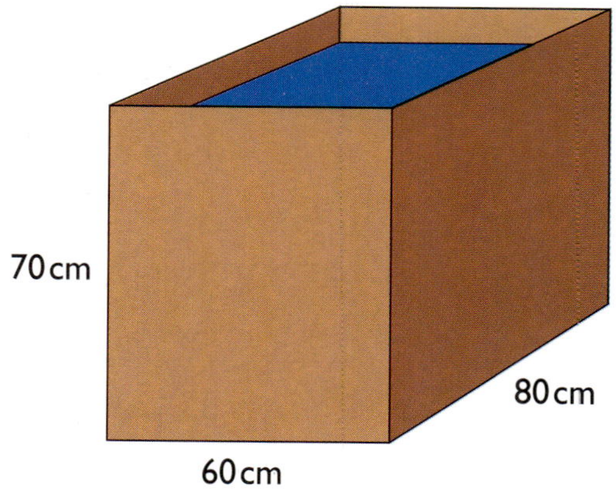

E The million challenges

E1 Challenge 1 – one million squares

This shows a piece of millimetre squared paper with one square millimetre highlighted in red.

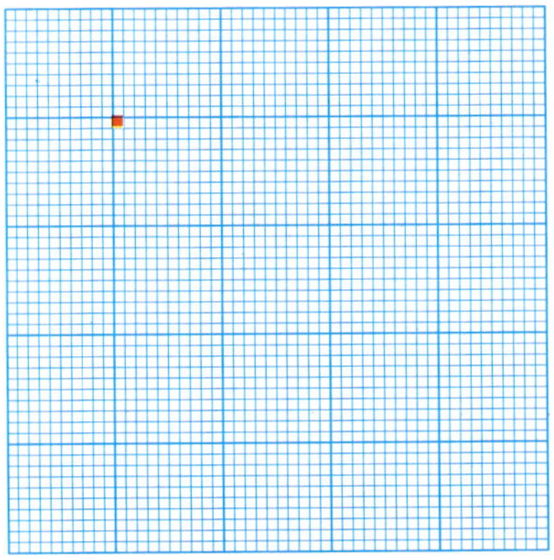

a Find the dimensions of a piece of paper which contains one million square millimetres.

b If a piece of A4 paper contains a millimetre grid with dimensions 190 mm by 280 mm, how many pieces of paper like this will be needed to make an area of 1 million square millimetres?

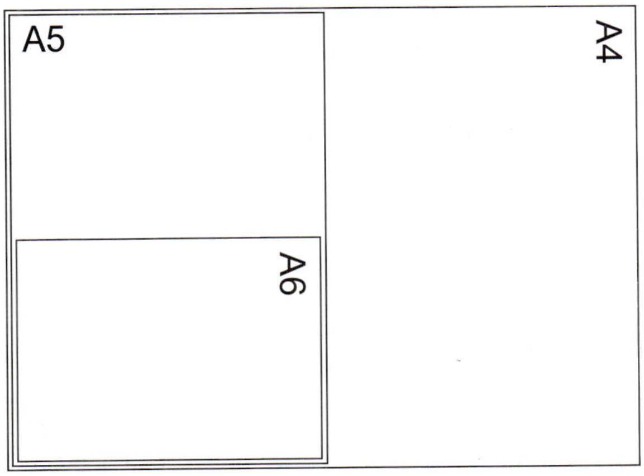

We often use A4 paper which is one of a series of international paper sizes. The smallest is A6 and the largest A0.

A6 is one half the size of A5
A5 is one half the size of A4 and so on.

c Will a grid containing one million 1 mm squares fit on to a sheet of A0 paper?

E2 Challenge 2 – capturing space

This picture illustrates one **cubic centimetre**.

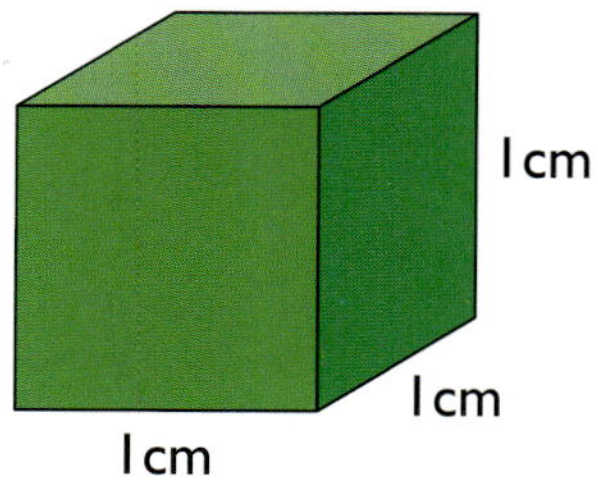

a Make or describe a cube which contains 1000 cubic centimetres.

b Make or describe a cube which contains one million cubic centimetres.

E3 Challenge 3 – a million paving slabs

A common size for the paving slabs used for footpaths is 90 cm x 60 cm.

They are usually used in tessellating patterns to cover large areas, sometimes in conjunction with 60 cm x 60 cm slabs, for example:

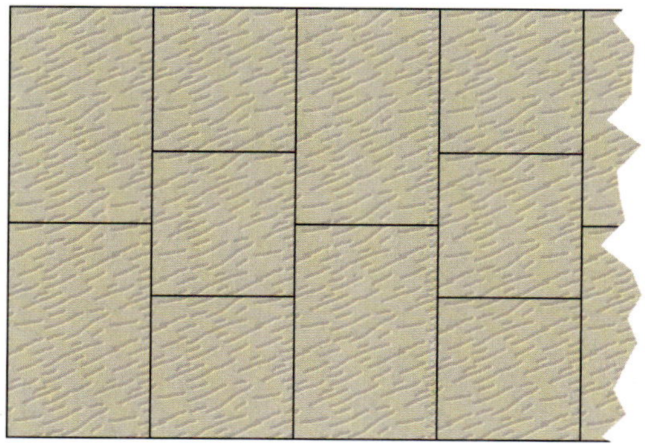

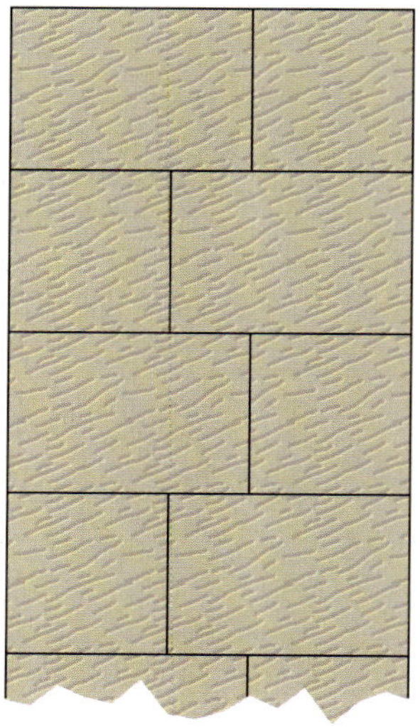

The challenge – what area would a million slabs cover?

A good way to describe a large area is to compare it with a familiar area such as a football pitch. The sizes of some common sports pitches are given on page 41. Choose one of these and calculate how many pitches would be covered by a million paving slabs, using the larger or smaller size or a combination of both sizes.

E4 Challenge 4 – finding millions around us

This is your challenge. Here are some ideas:

Think of a suitable unit, such as a second or a millimetre, and decide on a vivid way to describe what a million of them would look like.

For example, have you lived for a million seconds, or a million minutes or a million hours?

Do you travel a million millimetres on your way to school?

How heavy is a million grams?

Would a million grams of sugar fit on your desk or in your classroom or in your school?

A complete turn of a wheel is 360°. How many turns for 1 000 000°?

UNIT 9 Networks

A Routes

To get to school, Jasmine has to cross the road, go into the school grounds by a choice of gates or the hole in the fence and enter the building by one of three doors.

There are three approved ways of crossing the road: with the help of a 'lollipop lady', by zebra crossing and by traffic lights. On a quiet day, when there is no traffic, she realizes that she can cross without the help of these three ways. She now has four ways to cross the road.

A1 How many routes can she now take to get into school?

A mathematician looked at the same problem and drew this diagram:

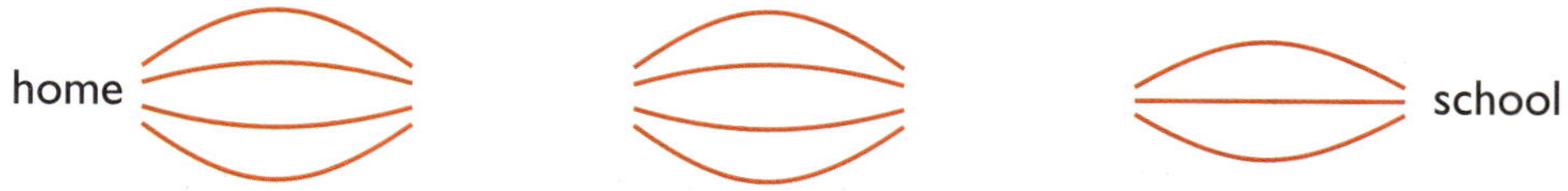

A2 Can you explain what the diagram means? (If not, read on.)

The first part of the drawing shows the four ways of crossing the road.

One line is the route across the zebra, one is the 'lollipop lady', one is using the traffic lights, and the fourth one is without any help.

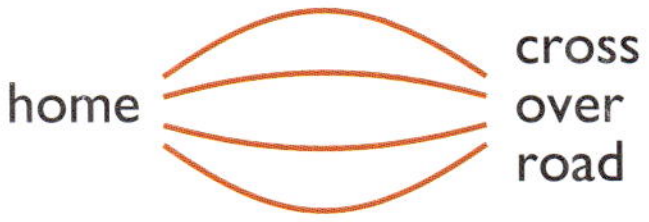

A3 Explain the meaning of the other two parts of the drawing.

The playing fields are across another road from a different part of the school.

To get to the playing fields, pupils must leave the school building by one of two side exits, go out of the school grounds by one of three gates, cross the road (no school crossing this time, but a zebra crossing and traffic lights), enter the playing fields by one of two gates or use a stile.

A4 How many different routes can pupils take to get out of the school grounds?

A5 Copy and complete this route diagram:

The first two stages help you to see if your answer to question **A4** was correct.

A6 How many different routes can pupils take to get from school to the playing fields? There are over 50, so before you start listing them, think about an easier way using the route diagram.

The previous question can be solved using a route diagram. Look at how many routes there are for each stage. To find the total number of possible routes, you multiply these together:

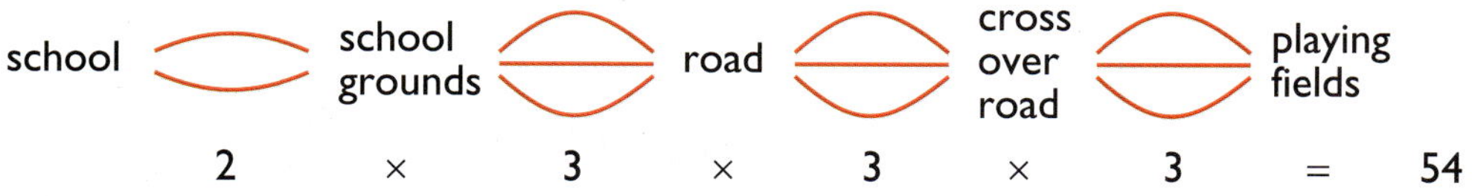

B Giving instructions

Coffee break

You are going to meet someone for coffee in a large new superstore. There are four different entrances.

There are two restaurants – the Snug Coffee Lounge and the Panorama Café.
Both serve coffee and both are on the 5th floor.
You can get there by lift, escalator or by stairs.

1st FLOOR	Ladies Fashions
2nd FLOOR	Household Furnishing
3rd FLOOR	Gents' Clothing
4th FLOOR	Books, Games, Toys
5th FLOOR	Snug Coffee Lounge Panorama Café

B1 Draw a route diagram showing all this information.

B2 Using the multiplication rule, work out the number of routes you can follow to have coffee at the superstore.

At the Snug Coffee Lounge, you see this special menu:

B3 How many different combinations can you have?

Draw a diagram like a route diagram to help you to find a solution.

The cinema

When you go to the cinema, how many decisions do you need to make?

Your decisions could be:

1. Do you go with your family, by yourself or with a friend?
2. Which of the four films will you see?
3. Do you buy an ice-cream or popcorn or sweets or a drink or nothing?
4. Do you go straight home or go to a coffee bar after the film?

B4 Draw a diagram, like a route diagram, to show these four decisions.

B5 Extend your diagram for question **B4** by adding the number of different routes you can take to reach the cinema.

Getting to school

When you go to school, how many decisions do you make?

Do you walk, go by bus, or car?

Do you take a different route on different days?

Where do you cross the road?

Which entrance do you use at school?

B6 Draw a route diagram to show all this information.

B7 How many different ways can you go to school?

B8 Which is the usual way that you go to school?

C Nodes and puzzles

C1 Which of these diagrams can you draw without taking your pencil off the paper and without going over any line twice?
Try to draw them in your exercise book.

a

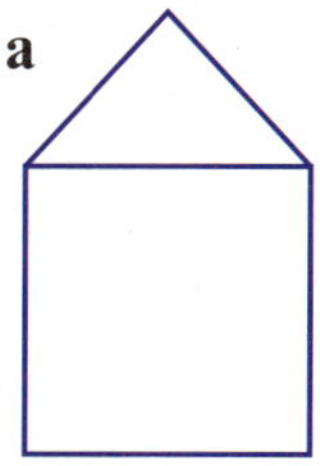

b

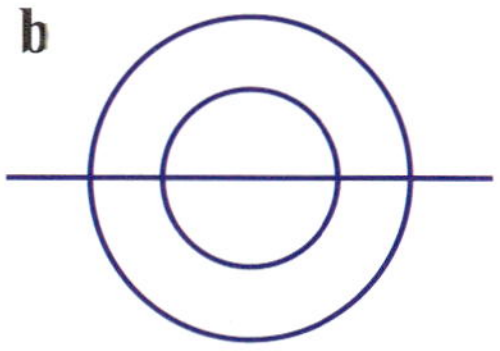

c

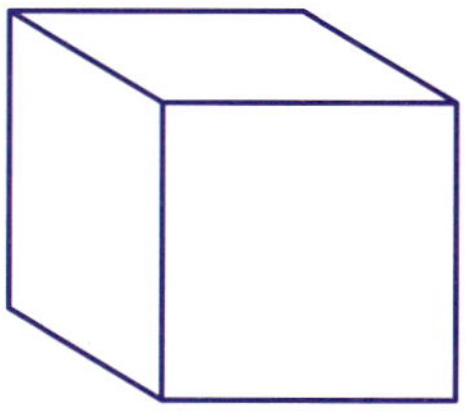

d

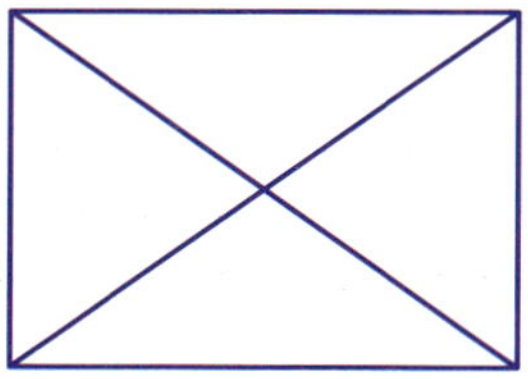

e

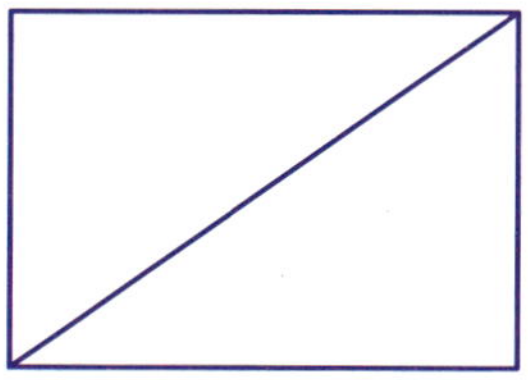

f

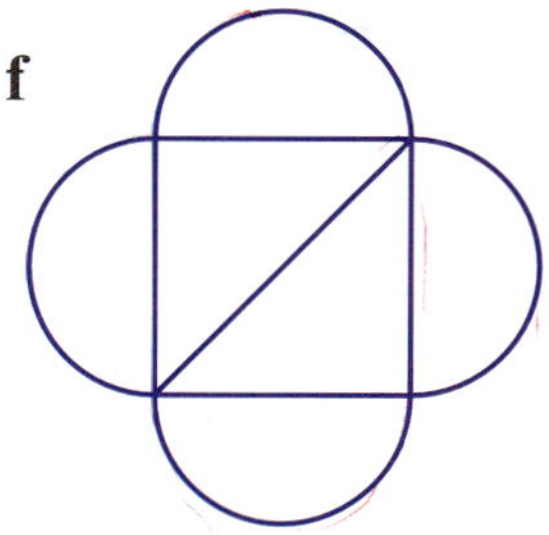

C2 Which of the diagrams are impossible to draw?

C3 How many different ways can you find for drawing the ones that are possible?

C4 Do you notice anything about the points where you start?

The six diagrams above are shown again on the next page.

Each junction or corner, called a **node**, has a dot and a letter.

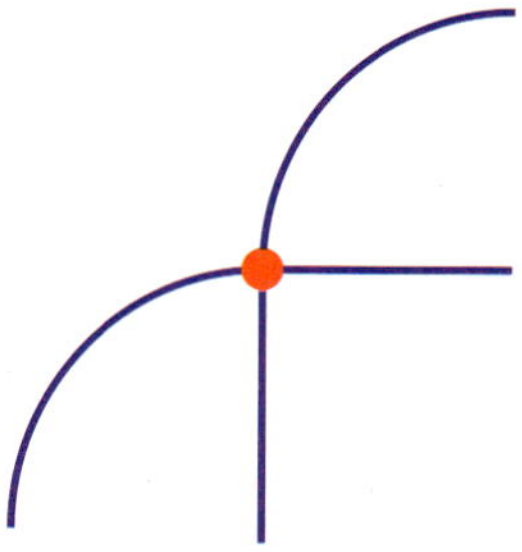

A node is where at least two routes meet.

The node shown here is where four routes meet.
This is called a node of order four.

The order of a node is the number of routes that meet at that point.

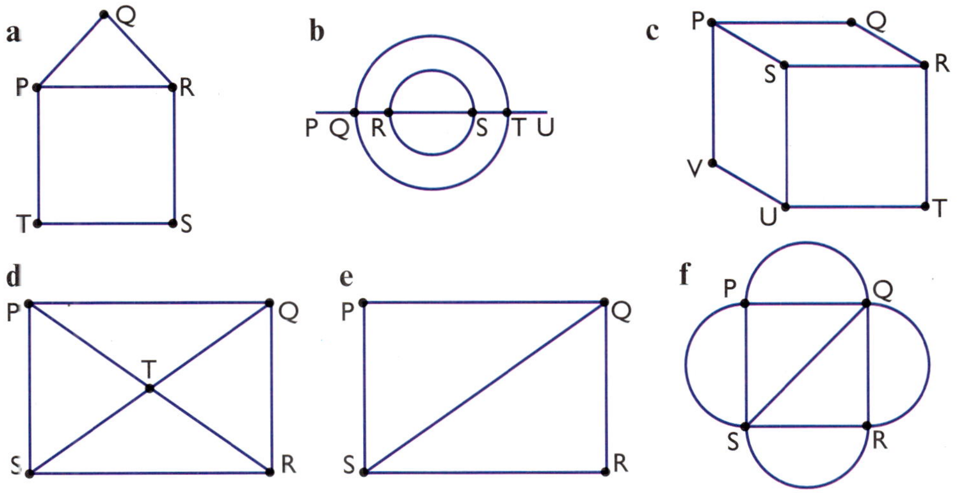

In diagram **a**, three routes meet at node P. That is, node P is order 3.

C5 Which other nodes are of order 3?

C6 How many nodes are of order 2?

C7 You need Worksheet S2:6. Copy and complete this table for each diagram.

C8 For each diagram that you were able to complete in question **C1**, circle the nodes where you started and finished. What do you notice about these?

Order of nodes in diagrams

Diagram / Node	a	b	c	d	e	f
P	3	1				
Q	2					
R	3					
S	2					
T	2					
U						
V						

C9 Now look in your completed table (question **C7**) at those diagrams which you were unable to draw. How many of the nodes were an order number which is odd?

If there are more than 2 nodes that have an order number which is odd, then the diagram is impossible to draw without taking your pencil off the paper or repeating a line twice.

C10 How many letters of the alphabet can you draw using the rules of question **C1**. (It may depend on the way you draw some of the letters.)

A B C D E F G H I J K L M N O P Q R S T U V W X Y Z

C11 Explain why it is impossible to draw A but you can draw P this way.

D The seven bridges of Königsberg

Königsberg was a town in Prussia which had seven bridges over the River Pregel. (It is now called Kaliningrad, in Russia, and has more bridges.)

D1 A well-known problem asks the question, 'Is it possible to take a walk, crossing all the bridges once only?'

Can you do it?

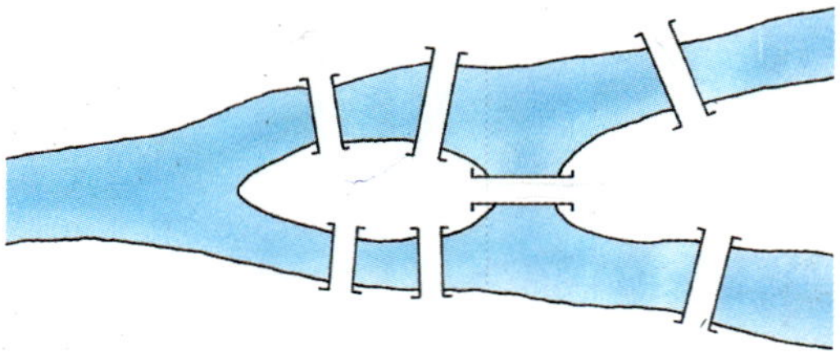

At the time it was set, the problem could not be solved.

But neither could it be shown that it was impossible.

This is a network diagram for the seven bridges.

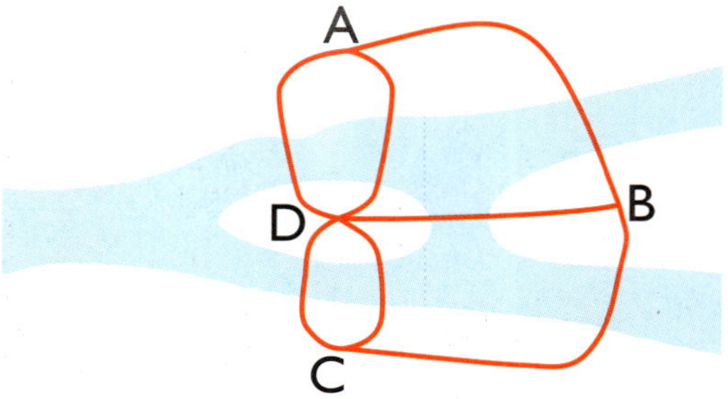

D2 Use this diagram to explain why it is impossible to cross all the bridges without crossing any bridge twice.

High wire

D3 The same ideas can be used with skeleton models of solids

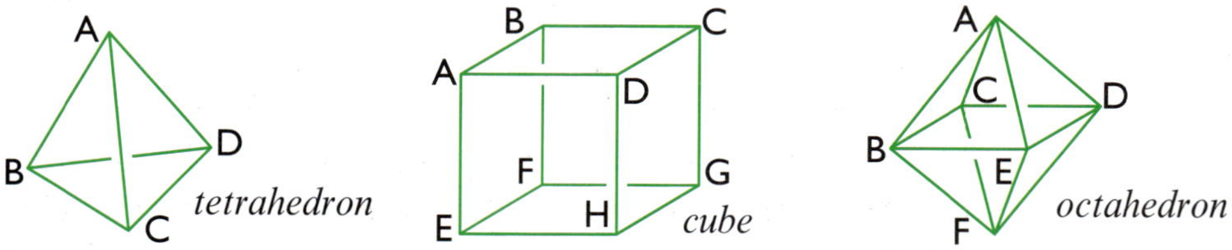

a The tetrahedron has been made out of 6 metres of wire (each edge is 1 metre). An ant starts at A and walks along the wire so that it does not walk along the same wire twice.
What is the greatest distance the ant can walk?

b A cube is made of 6 metres of wire. How long is each edge?
What is the greatest distance that another ant can walk if it starts at A and does not walk along the same edge twice? How can you be sure?

c The octahedron is also made of 6 metres of wire. What is the length of each edge? How far can the ant walk?

E Topology

So far, in this Unit, we have not been concerned with shape and distance. We have looked only at links and junctions in networks.

The study of this kind of geometry is called **topology**.

Topology can be very useful. The map of the London Underground tells us where to change trains and the order of stations on each line.

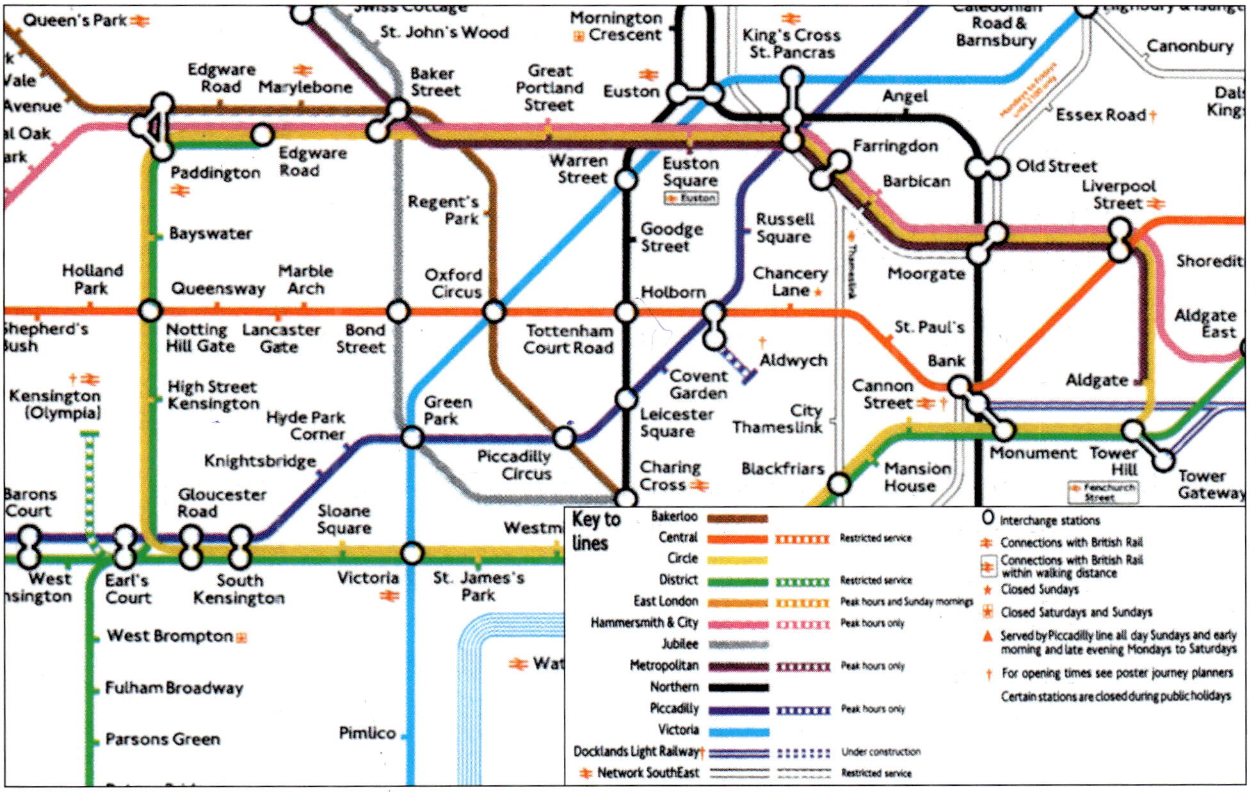

The red line represents the Central line. The stations on the Central line are indicated with a red mark but stations where you can change to another line are indicated with a circle. At Bond Street, for example, you can change to the Jubilee line.

E1 What two lines connect with the Central line at Oxford Circus?

E2 Write down three stations between Victoria and Euston on the Victoria line.

E3 Describe three different ways to travel from Notting Hill Gate to Piccadilly Circus.
Which is likely to be the quickest way? Why?

F The salesman's day

On a normal day, a salesman delivers to a shop in each of the towns in his area. It takes 15 minutes to unload at each shop. The time taken in minutes between towns is shown on the map.

F1 How long will he take to complete all deliveries if he follows the route B A C D E F G H I B?

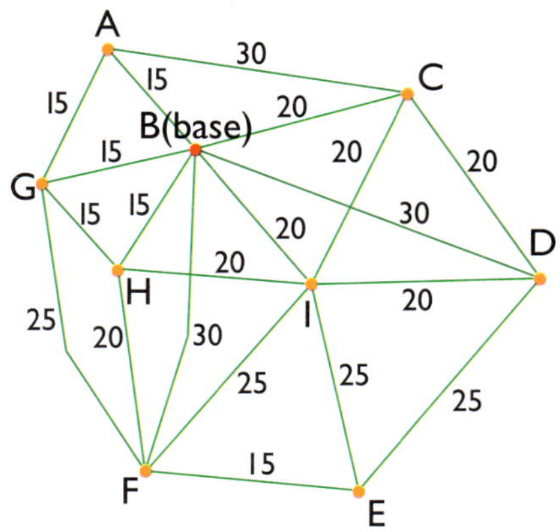

F2 Suggest another route which takes less time. Which is the quickest route?

F3 On Friday, he delivers for two days and his van is not big enough to contain all the stock he needs. He can do up to five deliveries before he needs to refill his van.

If it takes 30 minutes to load the van at base, how can he arrange to complete all his deliveries between 9 a.m. and 4 p.m.?

G Sprouts

Sprouts is a game for two players. You need scrap paper and a pencil.

scrap paper

Rules

1. On your paper, draw three nodes (points).
2. The first player joins one node to another and puts a new node in the middle of this line.
3. The next player now joins one node to another and puts a new node in the middle of this line.
4. The game continues, but no more than three lines can go from the same node. That is, no node can have an order higher than three.
5. The first person who cannot go is the loser.
6. Play the game again, but change who goes first. After playing a number of times, try a game with four or five nodes.

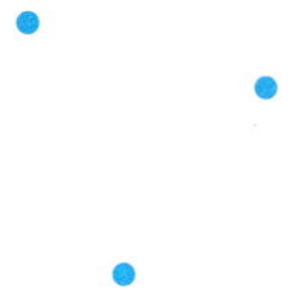

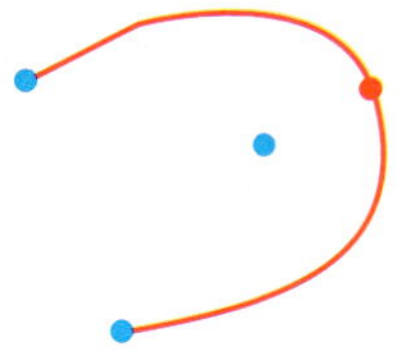

H Road networks

Motorways

The map shows the network of motorways in parts of the midlands and the north of England. The distances are in kilometres.

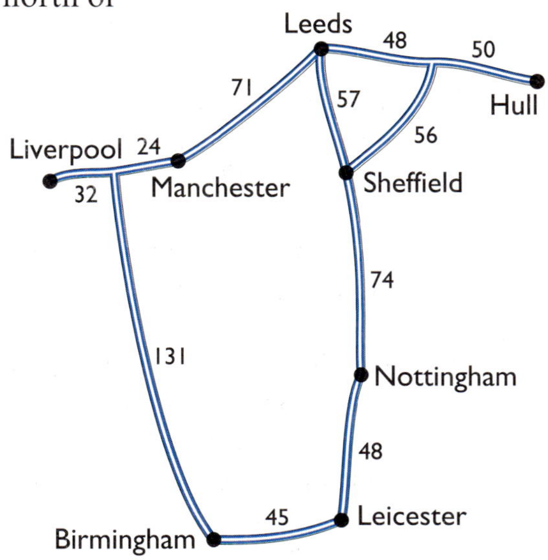

Answer the following questions from the map.

H1 How many kilometres is it from:

a Leicester to Nottingham

b Manchester to Leeds

c Hull to Manchester?

H2 On the shortest journey from Sheffield to Liverpool:

a list the major cities you would pass

b calculate the distance in kilometres.

H3 For a journey from Birmingham to Leeds:

a list two of the possible routes

b calculate the distance in kilometres for each route.

H4 Which city is 273 kilometres from Birmingham?

H5 If you start from Hull, list the shortest distances to all the other cities on the map. Put the cities in alphabetical order.

Shape, space and measure 2
National Curriculum level description coverage

NC level description	Covered in pupil's book unit:
• when constructing models and when drawing or using shapes, measure and draw angles to the nearest degree, and use language associated with angle	2, 4, 5, 7
• identify all the symmetries of 2-D shapes	3, 4, 5, 7
• know the rough metric equivalents of Imperial units still in daily use and convert one metric unit to another	6, 8
• make sensible estimates of a range of measures in relation to everyday situations	6, 8
• using and applying the above skills	All units

Important Note:
Although not specifically mentioned in the National Curriculum at this level, it is essential to cover basic work in area and volume (Unit 1).
Also, to provide a comprehensive education in geometry, we have included some work on networks and other topological areas (Unit 9).